# Families, Marriages, and Children

# Families, Marriages, and Children

## Charlotte Perkins Gilman

### Michael R. Hill, editor

Transaction Publishers
New Brunswick (U.S.A.) and London (U.K.)

Library of Congress Catalog Number: 2010015557
ISBN: 978-1-4128-1485-0
Printed in the United States of America

Library of Congress Cataloging-in-Publication Data

Gilman, Charlotte Perkins, 1860-1935.
 [Selections. 2010]
  Families, marriages, and children / Charlotte Perkins Gilman ; Michael R. Hill, editor.
    p. cm.
 Includes bibliographical references and index.
 ISBN 978-1-4128-1485-0
  1. Families. 2. Marriage. 3. Children. 4. Gilman, Charlotte Perkins, 1860-1935. I. Hill, Michael R. II. Title.

HQ518.G55    2010
306.874'3—dc22                               2010015557

*The editor happily dedicates this volume to Brian Patrick Conway, a perceptive sociologist, dedicated scholar, and convivial colleague.*

# Contents

Part IV:  Children and Parents

# Preface

It gives me enormous professional pleasure to present this unique collection of Gilman's writings on the sociology of marriages, families, children, and parenting to a wider audience of readers. This work, in its present form, came to life when Giuseppina Cersosimo accepted it for publication—in Italian translation—in her sociological series, *Esplorazioni* (published by Edizioni Kurumuny), where it will soon appear as *La sociologia della Famiglia. Matrimoni e figli.* I am delighted that Transaction Publications is now bringing forth these analyses for readers in Gilman's native language—English, thus making her insights easily available to new generations of students, scholars, and lay aficionados of perceptive social criticism.

Over the past several years, when designing and teaching sociology courses, I have found that assigning Gilman's shorter writings provides accessible and provocative introductions to numerous social issues that are sometimes thorny and contentious. This is especially true for the complex network of issues surrounding and defining marriage, family, and children's welfare. Whatever else Gilman does, she gets our attention and she makes us think. Gilman is a catalyst for dialogue, *par excellence.*

Friends, colleagues, and former students have encouraged me to edit and compile this volume, and for their comradeship I am deeply indebted. Throughout the development and execution of this work, my faith in sociology as a meaningful "calling" has been validated countless times in interactions with many people, including the intellectually adventurous students in the George Elliott Howard Seminars on Advanced Graduate Research in the Social Sciences, my tutees and professional colleagues in UNL's Hewit Center, my associates at *Sociological Origins*, every member of the Harriet Martineau Sociological Society, various champions of the ASA Section on the History of Sociology, and our delightful neighbors on Michigan's beautiful Mizpah Park Road. Bob Hunderfund masterfully transformed our lakeside cottage as this project unfolded, rescuing our venerable sanctuary in the nick of time. My life-partner, Mary Jo Deegan, makes everything possible—including love, space, and time for writing and research. For especially friendly smiles that brighten the long Nebraska winters, thanks always to June and Dave Bilyeu, Tom Carr, Miguel Carranza, Miguel Ceballos, Rollin Davis, Lavon and Bob Dye, Joleen Deats, James Free, Mary Jean Horst, Lori Ratzlaff, Charles Sayward, Sally and Bob Stoddard, and Morrie Tuttle. For salutary input on the present project, I particularly thank Giuseppina Cersosimo, Mary Jo Deegan, Kathleen Johnson, Jan Mach, Ann O'Hear, Raffaele Rauty, Deborah Ruigh, the convivial folks at Transaction, and the anonymous reviewers of the manuscript. The largest immediate debt, of course, belongs to Charlotte Perkins Gilman. I sincerely hope she would approve.

*—Michael R. Hill,*
*Lincoln, Nebraska*

# Introduction:
# Charlotte Perkins Gilman on the Sociology
# of Families, Marriages, and Children

Charlotte Perkins Gilman died in 1935, but she remains today a pro-vocative sociological writer; she makes us think, argue, and question our preconceptions, especially with regard to marriage and family. Several posthumous volumes of Gilman's work have been produced and it has been my pleasure to help present three of Gilman's (1997, 2002, 2004) major sociological writings to new generations of readers in English. As noted in the preface, it has been a special honor to acquaint an audience of Italian readers with a selection of her powerful writings on families, marriages, and children.[1] The present volume joins a small but growing collection of translations of Gilman's works into Italian. Gilman's classic work, *Women and Economics*, was early translated into Italian (1902), and is followed recently by translations of *The Yellow Wallpaper* (1976), *Herland* (1980), and a collection of tales (2008). An intriguing digital experiment is the new Italian thesaurus edition of *Our Androcentric Culture, or The Man-Made World* (2008). A recent book-length exposi-tion, in Italian, on Gilman's life and work is provided by Laura Moschini (2006). My goal for Italian readers, in selecting and editing the exemplars in the present volume, was to provide each reader with insightful and often trenchant examples of Gilman's sociological analyses and judg-ments about one of our most central social institutions: the family. Now, thanks to Transactions Publishers, these lively and insightful selections are also made more readily available to English readers.

Charlotte Perkins Gilman (1860-1935) was a pioneering sociologist, feminist pragmatist, author, and lecturer. She was born in Hartford, Con-necticut, and attended the Design College of Providence, Rhode Island. Her sociological education was largely self-taught. Gilman supported herself through writing and lecturing. She was a three-month resident and frequent visitor at Hull-House, Jane Addams' sociological settlement in Chicago, during 1895-96. Gilman was an active member of the American Sociological Association and presented papers at professional meetings of the association. One of her major accomplishments was the ability to explain sociological concepts and principles using the media of fiction and non-fiction alike.

## Reading Gilman from a Sociological Perspective

Gilman is not always easy to read—she can infuriate, astound, and perplex—but she always engages and often amuses her readers. Writing in an earlier time distinguished by different sensibilities and problems, Gilman brilliantly transcends her era and speaks insightfully to twenty-first-century readers about many lively social issues. Gilman's central strengths are her penetrating sociological analyses of marriage, mother-hood, and family relationships—the focus of the selections in this vol-ume. Gilman's wit, astute skill as a writer, and forthright language make her work especially accessible—and intriguing. Gilman never hides her conclusions behind sociological jargon, as do many writers today.

One key to understanding Gilman's work is to grasp her specifically sociological purpose and persona. Several full-length biographies and scholarly studies address Gilman's productive and controversial career, but—as they are written primarily by literary critics rather than social scientists—most fail miserably to articulate her work and perspective as a professional sociologist. A few American sociologists have recently rediscovered Gilman, and their analyses are, by contrast, cogent and ger-mane. The most penetrating is Mary Jo Deegan's (1997) lengthy essay on "Gilman's Sociological Journey from *Herland* to *Ourland*." Additional, specifically sociological interpretations of Gilman's work are found in: Clara Cahill Park (1936); Alice S. Rossi (1973); Bruce Keith (1991); my analytical synopsis of *Herland* (Hill, 1996); Patricia Lengerman and Jill Niebrugge-Brantly's (1998) chapter on Gilman; R.A. Sydie and Bert N. Adams' (2000) discussion in *Sociological Origins*; Hill and Deegan (2002, 2004); and my brief biographical sketch (Hill, 2007).

Gilman was a prolific and significant author. She is undoubtedly one of the more consequential women writers of the twentieth century and her (1892) semi-autobiographical story, "The Yellow Wall-Paper," is today one of the top-selling texts used in American literature courses across the USA. In all, Gilman wrote more than 2,000 published works, including the entire contents of each monthly issue of *The Forerunner*, a sociologically astute journal that she wrote, edited, and published from 1909 to 1916. It is a special treat that the selections in this volume, save one, are drawn from the difficult-to-find issues of *The Forerunner*. Gilman's many books and principal autobiographical materials include: *Women and Economics* (1898); *Concerning Children* (1900); *The Home* (1903); *Human Work* (1904); *The Man-Made World* (1911); *His Religion and Hers* (1923); a lively autobiography, *The Living of Charlotte Perkins Gilman* (1935); *Herland* (1979); *The Diaries of Charlotte Perkins Gilman* (1994); *A Journey from Within: The Love Letters of Charlotte Perkins Gilman, 1897-1900* (1995); *With Her in Ourland* (1997); *The Dress of Women* (2002); and *Social Ethics: Sociology and the Future of Society* (2004). For a useful and virtually complete bibliography, see Gary Scharnhorst's (1985) detailed compilation.

## Gilman's Challenges to Twenty-First Century Readers

Gilman challenges her readers on at least three temporal and theoretical levels. The first regards the continuing relevance of Gilman's analyses of past patterns to the lived realities of today. To what extent, and in what instances, do Gilman's empirical findings still hold without modification? The second concerns Gilman's forward-looking critiques, projections, and programmatic suggestions. In which specific cases, to date, has Gilman been proved wrong-headed or essentially correct? The third, and most important, level pertains to the viability of Gilman's overall theoretical framework. That is, if Gilman were alive and writing today, what would she logically conclude and instrumentally advise about the patterns of family, marriage, and motherhood that we currently observe? Do we find her conclusions helpful and practical? Each reader of this volume will find many passages that resonate and others that outrage, but the fundamental challenge is to assess Gilman's perspective as a constructive and progressive whole, to identify and evaluate the basic principles that give cohesion and coherence to her sociological vision.

The word choices made by Gilman a hundred years ago have not been altered in this volume, and this requires sensitivity and understanding on the part of the reader in two special instances. It behooves us to realize that when Gilman employed the terms "race" and "primitive" she was rarely ethnocentric, and never perversely bigoted. Gilman almost always employed "race" inclusively, to mean all "humanity" and "the human race" to reference all members of *homo sapiens*. In other instances, "race" refers to identifiable culture groups or societies having distinctive, recognized social patterns that may have been more or less enlightened, but *not* to erroneous presumptions about biological superiority or genetic inferiority. Today, Gilman would likely use alternative constructions and terminology to convey her intended meanings. Rather than refer to "the Japanese race," for example, she would likely mention "the Japanese people," or simply "the Japanese."

The term "primitive," as used by Gilman, refers simply to the reality that not all social groups possess the technological, medical, and scientific knowledge characteristic of "modern" societies. Gilman clearly affirms the potential for social progress and steadfastly opposes racial bigotry. She believed firmly in the fundamental humanity and brotherhood of all peoples. This does not mean, however, that she side-stepped her strongly felt obligation to criticize specific groups, cultures or institutionalized practices that she judged to be harmful, undemocratic, repressive, or reactionary.

Finally, a note on the editing and preparation of the essays in this book: With help from copyeditors at Transaction, I have corrected obvious typographical/typesetting errors that appeared in previously published versions. Similarly, punctuation is modernized in those places where the effect is unobtrusive and contributes to readability without impairing Gilman's distinctive style and cadence. The now peculiar time-bound spellings of Gilman's era, her archaic word choices, and her sometimes-dramatic use of capitalization are generally allowed to stand.

## Gilman on the Family

In writing about family as a core social institution, Gilman clearly understood that her readers' biases about family are likely deep and strong. When discussing the family, she observed:

> [W]e are confronted...with the most sensitive, powerful, universal, and ancient group of emotions known to man. This complex of feelings, tangled and knotted by ages of ironbound association; fired with the quenchless vitality of the biological necessities on which they rest; intensified by all our conscious centuries of social history; hallowed, sanctified, made imperative by recurrent religions; enforced with cruel penalties by law, and crueler ones by custom; first established by those riotous absurdities of dawning ethics, the sex-taboos of the primitive savage, and growing as a cult down all our ages of literature and art; the emotions, sentiments, traditions, race-habits, and fixed ideas which center in the home and family—form the most formidable obstacle to clear thought and wise conclusion.[2]

If, on first reading, the selections in this volume seem puzzling or difficult to comprehend, it is worth asking if the underlying problem may lie, at least in part, with the reader's unexamined defenses against ideas that challenge his/her deepest emotions and cultural biases.

## The Organization of This Volume

The selections in this volume are arbitrarily divided into four thematic groups. While each selection is distinctive, each links conceptually into Gilman's wider understanding of society, family, marriage, and children. For Gilman, patriarchal thinking too often prevents the family *as a social pattern* from contributing constructively to the wider social good. The home is anchored in a massive nexus of institutional patterns wherein traditional male prerogatives have significant consequences for everyday life in families. In order to improve family life, Gilman argues, it is necessary to reform the overall society in which families exist. These results are interactive and cumulative, Gilman hypothesizes. Thus, better family life leads, in turn, to a more humane and progressive society. Within her general framework, the following themes may be discerned.

*Family, Home, and Society*

Today's family, posits Gilman, is not so much a naturally-occurring pattern of social organization as it is a distinctly *man*-made institution that privileges men over women (selection 1). Males, Gilman asserts, have usurped the original matriarchal basis of society; the family, as a social institution has been reshaped for the direct and continuing benefit of patriarchal men. In Gilman's 1909 address to her colleagues in the American Sociological Society (selection 2), she outlines the social factors that affect the home which, in turn, affect the family. Of special interest to Gilman are what she calls (1) the "material" (or physical and economic) aspects of society and (2) the role or position of women in society as a whole. In societies where large numbers of women live in poverty and/or affluence, in separately organized domiciles, the result for children is dreadful. This selection reveals Gilman as a professional sociological theorist talking frankly with her peers.

In an imaginative sociological parable on "ancestors" (selection 3), Gilman conducts a sociological thought experiment in which the main protagonist looks back through time to see *all* of his distant family relations. Tracing one's "roots" is a serious passion for many genealogists, a religious issue for members of the Church of Latter Day Saints, and a source of pride for members of organizations like the Daughters of the American Revolution. But, is it right to base social acceptance on who a person's ancestors were? Who counts as "family"? Who counts as "kin"? How far back should we look? We are better off looking forward—Gilman suggests—to the future.

During Gilman's era, the majority of American families still lived in rural settings, and married women were likely wives of farmers. Thus, Gilman addresses the social and economic realities confronting farm wives, a distinctly oppressed group within a generally wealthier and rapidly industrializing, increasingly urban society (selection 4). Here, Gilman argues for widespread collective action on the part of women, primarily for the purpose of better realizing their duties to their children. With the present shift to a fully urbanized society, Gilman would now more directly address her city sisters, but she would likely argue that two things have not changed: (1) the rural countryside remains the best environment in which to raise children, and (2) the economic desperation and social isolation of farm wives, however many fewer in number today, continues largely unabated.

*Men and Marriage*

Life can be lived by women without a husband (selection 10), as a spinster or a widow, for example, but for most women marriage—to a man—is the norm, and is the primary means by which families are created. Thus, women who want children typically become institutionally entangled with men via marriage, often with momentous consequences. By asking, and answering, the question: Does a man support his wife? (selection 5) Gilman draws us squarely into the internal economics of the modern household. Does it make sense in an industrialized world—where most people generate income as wage earners—for husbands, but not wives, to be the only family members with paying jobs? Gilman asks this question from the viewpoints of (1) society as a whole and (2) the individual family as a domestic unit. Does a housewife's unpaid labor contribute to the community or injure it economically? To provide an answer to this surprisingly complex question, Gilman takes us step by step through the economics of everyday life, including an analysis of the money economy in a hypothetical woman-centered household. Gilman concludes that monetary dependency, whether between men, between two women, or between a man and a woman, is seriously problematic, not only for each couple but also for society generally.

Families are distinguished, one from the other, by surnames (selections 6 and 11). These names, Gilman observes, are the names of *men*—fathers and husbands. Despite the presumed advances in women's rights achieved since Gilman's analysis in 1911, including the use of "Ms."

and some women who keep their maiden names when married, the ponderous fact still remains that the surname for virtually all women in American society is a patronym, a name derived from a father rather than a mother. Note, for the record, that Gilman had three patronyms at various times: Charlotte *Perkins* (her maiden name), Charlotte Perkins *Stetson* (her first husband's surname), and ultimately Charlotte Perkins *Gilman* (her second husband's surname). Gilman succinctly and poignantly catalogues the differential advantages men enjoy by virtue of always having the same family surname.

For Gilman, marriage should be a partnership of equals. Nonetheless, our patriarchal society privileges the male partner in heterosexual unions. Socially, women are defined as "competing" with men (selection 8) and as requiring alimony (as distinct from child-support) when marriages dissolve in divorce (section 7). Men, Gilman shows, are lionized for being prolific "fathers," whereas women largely earn obscurity as "mothers" (selection 9). If motherhood is to achieve its rightful due, then society and marriage must be radically transformed.

## Motherhood

Throughout the readings in this volume (and especially in selections 12-15), Gilman posits that children deserve better care and attention than can be provided by "average" women who are untrained in the principles of right motherhood. Gilman employs the concept of "social parentage" and contrasts this idea with notions of parenthood rooted in the traditions of previous eras. Motherhood and children should receive priority, she argues, but not in self-defeating ways that preserve outdated and injurious inequities between husbands and wives. As a sociologist, Gilman's concrete, practical words of instruction give solid support to politicians who campaign on platforms of "putting children and families first." Gilman presents a powerful brief for her version of the New Motherhood.

## Children and Parents

The most significant activity assigned to marriage, family, and home as enduring social patterns is the biological reproduction, early care, and socialization of children (selections 16-20). Birth and death are dynamic transitions in human life. Husbands and wives become mothers and fathers, widows and widowers. Children become siblings and orphans.

Sons and daughters become heads of families, caretakers, and executors. Children are born into potentially large networks of pre-existing family relationships not only with parents and siblings, but also with grandparents, aunts, uncles, and cousins of various degrees. Through the mechanism of human reproduction, society not only reproduces itself but also opens the door to social transformation and renewal. For Gilman, children are literally our future, and thus we must take extraordinary care to rear our children wisely.

What should be the fate of children who, by definition, have no control over the social situations into which they are born? Gilman argues that no child should suffer, even if the parents make mistakes. Gilman's general solution is to radically improve the economic, political, and educational status of women. If a woman has a child out of wedlock, she should be able to raise her baby in a loving home free of economic want. Similarly, a pregnant young wife whose husband is suddenly killed in an accident should be able to support herself and her soon-to-be-born child. Gilman examines the concept of "illegitimacy" (selection 18), traces its roots, and argues for a society in which children are not damned by their parents' errors, for a society in which changes in longstanding, fundamental social patterns are not only desirable but are also possible. Gilman's prediction that "bastard," as a socially significant category, if not as a derogatory epithet, would be eliminated has been slowly realized. Finally, Gilman asks, "Is childhood happy?" (selection 20). Not generally, she concludes, but it can become so.

## Conclusion

Gilman believed deeply that women's values make for better societies. Whereas men's values are destructive, competitive, and often violent, women embrace regeneration, cooperation, and compassion. Each family is a microcosm of society in which these values struggle for recognition and acceptance. Patriarchal families necessarily produce double standards and inequalities between husbands and wives, resulting in inferior mothers and, as a direct consequence, substandard children. To improve society, we need healthy, happy children. The latter requires well-trained, competent mothers, widespread social parenting, and enlightened, non-patriarchal marriages. This is Gilman's social program and comprises the theme that runs without apology through all of the selections in this volume.

*—Michael R. Hill*

# References

## Works in Italian

Gilman, Charlotte Perkins. 1902. *La donna e l'economia sociale: studio delle relazioni economiche fra uomini e donne e della loro azione nell'evoluzione sociale.* [Women and Economics: A Study of the Economic Relation between Men and Women as a Factor in Social Evolution]. Firenze: G. Barbèra.
_____. 1976. *La cara gialla.* [The Yellow Wallpaper]. Milana: La Tartaruga.
_____. 1980. *Terradilei.* [The Yellow Wallpaper *and* Herland]. Milano: Tartaruga.
_____. 2008. *Racconti de silenzi e di anarchie.* [Tales of Silence and Anarchy]. Translated by M. Romeo. [Place not stated]: Quattrosoli.
Moschini, Laura. 2006. *Charlotte Perkins Gilman: La straordinaria vita di una femminista vittoriana.* [Charlotte Perkins Gilman: The Extraordinary Life of a Victorian Feminist]. Roma: Aracne.

## Digital Edition in English with Digital Thesaurus in Italian

Gilman, Charlotte Perkins. 2008. *Our Androcentric Culture: or The Man-Made World.* Webster's Italian Thesaurus edition. ISBN 019135001. Retrieved January 22, 2009, from www.lauriejbooks.com

## Works in English

Deegan, Mary Jo. 1997. "Gilman's Sociological Journey from *Herland* to *Ourland*." Pp. 1-57 in *With Her in Ourland: Sequel to Herland*, by Charlotte Perkins Gilman, edited by Mary Jo Deegan and Michael R. Hill. Westport, CT: Greenwood/Praeger.
Deegan, Mary Jo and Christopher W. Podeschi. 2001. "The Ecofeminist Pragmatism of Charlotte Perkins Gilman." *Environmental Ethics* 23 (Spring): 19-36.
Gilman, Charlotte Perkins. 1892. "The Yellow Wall-Paper." *New England Magazine*, new series 3 (September): 134-135.
_____. 1898. *Women and Economics: A Study of the Economic Relation between Men and Women as a Factor in Social Evolution.* Boston: Small, Maynard. (Reprinted with an introduction by Carl N. Degler. New York: Harper and Row, 1966).
_____. 1900. *Concerning Children.* Boston: Small, Maynard.
_____. 1903. *The Home: Its Work and Influences.* New York: McClure and Phillips.
_____. 1904. *Human Work.* New York: McClure and Phillips.
_____, (Ed.). 1909-1916. *The Forerunner.* New York: Charlotte Perkins Gilman.
_____. 1911. *The Man-Made World, or Our Androcentric Culture.* London: T. Fisher Unwin.
_____. 1923. *His Religion and Hers: A Study of the Faith of Our Fathers and the Work of Our Mothers.* New York: Century.
_____. 1935 *The Living of Charlotte Perkins Gilman: An Autobiography.* With a foreword by Zona Gale. New York: D. Appleton-Century.
_____. 1979. *Herland.* Introduced by Ann J. Lane. New York: Pantheon. (Originally published in *The Forerunner*, 1915).
_____. 1994. *The Diaries of Charlotte Perkins Gilman.* Edited by Denise D. Knight. Charlottesville: University Press of Virginia.
_____. 1995. *A Journey from Within: The Love Letters of Charlotte Perkins Gilman, 1897-1900.* Edited by Mary A. Hill. Lewisburg, PA: Bucknell University Press.

_____. 1997a. *With Her in Ourland: Sequel to Herland.* Edited by Mary Jo Deegan and Michael R. Hill. Westport, CT: Greenwood. (Originally published in *The Forerunner*, 1916).

_____. 2002. *The Dress of Women: A Critical Introduction to the Symbolism and Sociology of Clothing.* Edited by Michael R. Hill and Mary Jo Deegan. Westport, CT: Greenwood. (Originally published in *The Forerunner*, 1915).

_____. 2004. *Social Ethics: Sociology and the Future of Society.* Edited by Michael R. Hill and Mary Jo Deegan. Westport, CT: Praeger. (Originally published in *The Forerunner*, 1914).

Hill, Michael R. 1996. "*Herland,* by Charlotte Perkins Gilman." Pp. 251-54 in *Masterpieces of Women's Literature,* edited by Frank N. Magill. New York: HarperCollins.

_____. 2007. "Charlotte Perkins Gilman." Pp. 1941-1942 in the *Blackwell Encyclopedia of Sociology,* Vol. 4, edited by George Ritzer. Malden, MA: Blackwell Publishing.

Hill, Michael R. and Mary Jo Deegan. 2002. "Charlotte Perkins Gilman on the Symbolism and Sociology of Clothing." Pp. ix-xxvii in *The Dress of Women: A Critical Introduction to the Symbolism and Sociology of Clothing,* by Charlotte Perkins Gilman, edited by Michael R. Hill and Mary Jo Deegan. Westport, CT: Greenwood Press.

_____. 2004. "Charlotte Perkins Gilman's Sociological Perspective on Ethics and Society." Pp. vix-xxvii in *Social Ethics: Sociology and the Future of Society,* by Charlotte Perkins Gilman, edited by Michael R. Hill and Mary Jo Deegan. Westport, CT: Praeger.

Keith, Bruce. 1991. "Charlotte Perkins Gilman (1860-1935)." Pp. 148-156 in *Women in Sociology: A Bio-Bibliographical Sourcebook,* edited by Mary Jo Deegan. New York: Greenwood Press.

Lengermann, Patricia Madoo and Jill Niebrugge-Brantley. 1998. "Charlotte Perkins Gilman (1860-1935)—Gender and Social Structure." Pp. 105-130 in *The Women Founders: Sociology and Social Theory, 1830-1930: A Text/Reader,* edited by Patrica Madoo Lengermann and Jill Niebrugge-Brantley. Boston: McGraw-Hill.

Park, Clara Cahill. 1936. Review of *The Living of Charlotte Perkins Gilman,* by Charlotte Perkins Gilman. *American Journal of Sociology* 41 (May): 701-702.

Rossi, Alice S. 1973. "The Militant Madonna: Charlotte Perkins Gilman." Pp. 566-572 in *The Feminist Papers,* edited by Alice S. Rossi. New York: Columbia University Press.

Scharnhost, Gary. 1985. *Charlotte Perkins Gilman: A Bibliography.* Metuchen, NJ: Scarecrow.

Sydie, R.A. and Bert N. Adams. 2000. "Beatrice Webb and Charlotte Perkins Gilman: Feminist Debates and Contradictions." *Sociological Origins* 2 (Summer): 5-14.

# Notes

1.  This edited volume of Gilman's work was originally prepared at the request of Giuseppina Cersosimo who directs the Italian sociological series, *Esplorazioni,* published by Edizioni Kurumuny. It will soon appear—in Italian translation—as *La sociologia della Famiglia. Matrimoni e figli.*

2.  Quoted from Gilman's 1909 address to the American Sociological Society, selection 2, below.

# Part I

## Family, Home, and Society

# 1

# The Man-Made Family (1909)

The family is older than humanity, and therefore cannot be called a human institution.[1] A post office, now, is *wholly* human; no other creature has a postoffice, but there are families in plenty among birds and beasts; all kinds permanent and transient; monogamous, polygamous, and polyandrous.[2]

We are now to consider the growth of the family in humanity; What is its rational development in humanness; in mechanical, mental and social lines; in the extension of love and service; and the effect upon it of this strange new arrangement—a masculine proprietor.

Like all natural institutions the family has a purpose; and is to be measured primarily as it serves that purpose; which is, the care and nurture of the young. To protect the helpless little ones, to feed and shelter them, to ensure them the benefits of an ever longer period of immaturity, and so to improve the race—this is the original purpose of the family.

When a natural institution becomes human it enters the plane of consciousness. We think about it; and, in our strange new power of voluntary action do things to it. We have done strange things to the family; or, more specifically, men have.

Balsac, at his bitterest, observed, "Woman's virtue is man's best invention."[3] Balsac was wrong. Virtue—the unswerving devotion to one mate—is common among birds and some of the higher mammals. If Balsac meant celibacy when he said virtue, why that is one of man's inventions—though hardly his best.

What man has done to the family, speaking broadly, is to change it from an institution for the best service of the child to one modified to his own service, the vehicle of his comfort, power, and pride.

Among the heavy millions of the unstirred East, a child—necessarily a male child—is desired for the credit and glory of the father, and his fathers; in place of seeing that all a parent is for is the best service of the child. Ancestor worship, that gross reversal of all natural law, is of wholly androcentric origin. It is strongest among old patriarchal races; lingers on in feudal Europe; is to be traced even in America today in a few sporadic efforts to magnify the deeds of our ancestors.

The best thing any of us can do for our ancestors is to be better than they were; and we ought to give our minds to it. When we use our past merely as a guidebook, and concentrate our noble emotions on the present and future, we shall improve more rapidly.

The peculiar changes brought about in family life by the predominance of the male are easily traced. In these studies we must keep clearly in mind the basic masculine characteristics; desire, combat, self-expression; all legitimate and right in proper use: only mischievous when excessive or out of place. Through them the male is led to strenuous competition for the favor of the female; in the overflowing ardors of song, as in nightingale and tom-cat; in wasteful splendor of personal decoration, from the pheasant's breast to an embroidered waistcoat; and in direct struggle for the prize, from the stag's locked horns to the clashing spears of the tournament.

It is earnestly hoped that no reader will take offence at the necessarily frequent reference to these essential features of maleness. In the many books about women it is, naturally, their femaleness that has been studied and enlarged upon. And though women, after thousands of years of such discussion, have become a little restive under the constant use of the word female: men, as rational beings, should not object to an analogous study—at least not for some time—a few centuries or so.

How, then, do we find these masculine tendencies, desire, combat, and self-expression, affect the home and family when given too much power?

First comes the effect in the preliminary work of selection. One of the most uplifting forces of nature is that of sex selection. The males, numerous, varied, pouring a flood of energy into wide modifications, compete for the female, and she selects the victor; this securing to the race the new improvements.

In forming the proprietary family there is no such competition, no such selection. The man, by violence or by purchase, does the choosing—he selects the kind of woman that pleases him. Nature did not intend him to select; he is not good at it. Neither was the female intended to compete—she is not good at it.

If there is a race between males for a mate—the swiftest gets her first; but if one male is chasing a number of females, he gets the slowest first. The one method improves our speed: the other does not. If males struggle and fight with one another for a mate, the strongest secures her; if the male struggles and fights with the female—(a peculiar and unnatural horror, known only among human beings) he most readily secures the weakest. The one method improves our strength—the other does not.

When women became the property of men; sold and bartered; "given away" by their paternal owner to their marital owner; they lost this prerogative of the female, this primal duty of selection. The males were no longer improved by their natural competition for the female; and the females were not improved; because the male did not select for points of racial superiority, but for such qualities as pleased him.

There is a locality in northern Africa, where young girls are deliberately fed with a certain oily seed, to make them fat—that they may be the more readily married—as the men like fat wives. Among certain more savage African tribes the chief's wives are prepared for him by being kept in small dark huts and fed on "mealies" and molasses; precisely as a Strasbourg goose is fattened for the gourmand. Now fatness is not a desirable race characteristic; it does not add to the woman's happiness or efficiency; or to the child's; it is merely an accessory pleasant to the master; his attitude being much as the amorous monad ecstatically puts it, in Sill's[4] quaint poem, "Five Lives,"

"O the little female monad's lips!
O the little female monad's eyes!
O the little, little, female, female monad!"

This ultra littleness and ultra femaleness has been demanded and produced by our Androcentric Culture.

Following this, and part of it, comes the effect on motherhood. This function was the original and legitimate base of family life; and its ample sustaining power throughout the long early period of "the mother-right;" or as we call it, the matriarchate; the father being her assistant in the great work. The patriarchate, with its proprietary family, changed this altogether; the woman, as the property of the man was considered first and foremost as a means of pleasure to him; and while she was still valued as a mother, it was in a tributary capacity. Her children were now his; his property, as she was; the whole enginery of the family was turned from its true use to this new one, hitherto unknown, the service of the adult male.

To this day we are living under the influence of the proprietary family. The duty of the wife is held to involve man-service as well as child-service; and indeed far more; as the duty of the wife to the husband quite transcends the duty of the mother to the child.

See, for instance, the English wife staying with her husband in India and sending the children home to be brought up; because India is bad for children. See our common law that the man decides the place of residence; if the wife refuses to go with him to howsoever unfit a place for her and for the little ones, such refusal on her part constitutes "desertion" and is ground for divorce.

See again the idea that the wife must remain with the husband though a drunkard, or diseased; regardless of the sin against the child involved in such a relation. Public feeling on these matters is indeed changing; but as a whole the ideals of the man-made family still obtain.

The effect of this on the woman has been inevitably to weaken and overshadow her sense of the real purpose of the family; of the relentless responsibilities of her duty as a mother. She is first taught duty to her parents, with heavy religious sanction; and then duty to her husband, similarly buttressed; but her duty to her children has been left to instinct. She is not taught in girlhood as to her preeminent power and duty as a mother; her young ideals are all of devotion to the lover and husband, with only the vaguest sense of results.

The young girl is reared in what we call "innocence"; poetically described as "bloom"; and this condition is held to be one of her chief "charms." The requisite is wholly androcentric. This "innocence" does not enable her to choose a husband wisely; she does not even know the dangers that possibly confront her. We vaguely imagine that her father or brother, who do know, will protect her. Unfortunately, the father and brother, under our current "double standard" of morality, do not judge the applicants as she would if she knew the nature of their offenses.

Furthermore, if her heart is set on one of them, no amount of general advice and opposition serves to prevent her marrying him. "I love him!" she says, sublimely. "I do not care what he has done. I will forgive him. I will save him!"

This state of mind serves to forward the interests of the lover, but is of no advantage to the children. We have magnified the duties of the wife, and minified the duties of the mother; and this is inevitable in a family relation every law and custom of which is arranged from the masculine viewpoint.

From this same viewpoint, equally essential to the proprietary family, comes the requirement that the woman shall serve the man. Her service is not that of the associate and equal, as when she joins him in his business. It is not that of a beneficial combination, as when she practices another business and they share the profits; it is not even that of the specialist, as the service of a tailor or barber; it is personal service—the work of a servant.

In large generalization, the women of the world cook and wash, sweep and dust, sew and mend, for the men.

We are so accustomed to this relation; have held it for so long to be the "natural" relation, that it is difficult indeed to show that it is distinctly unnatural and injurious. The father expects to be served by the daughter, a service quite different from what he expects of the son. This shows at once that such service is no integral part of motherhood, or even of marriage; but is supposed to be the proper industrial position of women, as such.

Why is this so? Why, on the face of it, given a daughter and a son, should a form of service be expected of the one, which would be considered ignominious by the other?

The underlying reason is this. Industry, at its base, is a feminine function. The surplus energy of the mother does not manifest itself in noise, or combat, or display, but in productive industry. Because of her mother-power she became the first inventor and laborer; being in truth the mother of all industry as well as all people.

Man's entrance upon industry is late and reluctant; as will be shown later in treating his effect on economics. In this field of family life, his effect was as follows:

Establishing the proprietary family at an age when the industry was primitive and domestic; and thereafter confining the woman solely to the domestic area, he thereby confined her to primitive industry. The domestic industries, in the hands of women, constitute a survival of our remotest past. Such work was "woman's work" as was all the work then known; such work is still considered woman's work because they have been prevented from doing any other.

The term "domestic industry" does not define a certain kind of labor, but a certain grade of labor. Architecture was a domestic industry once—when every savage mother set up her own tepee. To be confined to domestic industry is no proper distinction of womanhood; it is an historic distinction, an economic distinction, it sets a date and limit to woman's industrial progress.

In this respect the man-made family has resulted in arresting the development of half the world. We have a world wherein men, industrially, live in the twentieth century; and women, industrially, live in the first—and back of it.

To the same source we trace the social and educational limitations set about women. The dominant male, holding his women as property, and fiercely jealous of them, considering them always as *his*, not belonging to themselves, their children, or the world; has hedged them in with restrictions of a thousand sorts; physical, as in the crippled Chinese lady[5] or the imprisoned odalisque[6]; moral, as in the oppressive doctrines of submission taught by all our androcentric religions; mental, as in the enforced ignorance from which women are now so swiftly emerging.

This abnormal restriction of women has necessarily injured motherhood. The man, free, growing in the world's growth, has mounted with the centuries, filling an ever wider range of world activities. The woman, bound, has not so grown; and the child is born to a progressive fatherhood and a stationary motherhood. Thus the man-made family reacts unfavorably upon the child. We rob our children of half their social heredity by keeping the mother in an inferior position; however legalized, hallowed, or ossified by time, the position of a domestic servant is inferior.

It is for this reason that child culture is at so low a level, and for the most part utterly unknown. Today, when the forces of education are steadily working nearer to the cradle, a new sense is wakening of the importance of the period of infancy, and its wiser treatment; yet those who know of such a movement are few, and of them some are content to earn easy praise—and pay—by belittling right progress to gratify the prejudices of the ignorant.

The whole position is simple and clear; and easily traceable to its root. Given a proprietary family, where the man holds the woman primarily for his satisfaction and service—then necessarily he shuts her up and keeps her for these purposes. Being so kept, she cannot develop humanly, as he has, through social contact, social service, true social life. (We may note in passing, her passionate fondness for the child-game called "society" she has been allowed to entertain herself withal; that poor simiacrum[7] of real social life, in which people decorate themselves and madly crowd together, chattering, for what is called "entertainment"). Thus checked in social development, we have but a low-grade motherhood to offer our children; and the children, reared in the primitive conditions thus artificially maintained, enter life with a false perspective, not only toward men and women, but toward life as a whole.

The child should receive in the family, full preparation for his relation to the world at large. His whole life must be spent in the world, serving it well or ill; and youth is the time to learn how. But the androcentric home cannot teach him. We live today in a democracy—the man-made family is a despotism. It may be a weak one; the despot may be dethroned and overmastered by his little harem of one; but in that case she becomes the despot—that is all. The male is esteemed "the head of the family"; it belongs to him; he maintains it; and the rest of the world is a wide hunting ground and battlefield wherein he competes with other males as of old.

The girl-child, peering out, sees this forbidden field as belonging wholly to men-kind; and her relation to it is to secure one for herself—not only that she may love, but that she may live. He will feed, clothe, and adorn her—she will serve him; from the subjection of the daughter to that of the wife she steps; from one home to the other, and never enters the world at all—man's world.

The boy, on the other hand, considers the home as a place of women, an inferior place, and longs to grow up and leave it—for the real world. He is quite right. The error is that this great social instinct, calling for full social exercise, exchange, service, is considered masculine, whereas it is human, and belongs to boy and girl alike.

The child is affected first through the retarded development of his mother, then through the arrested condition of home industry; and further through the wrong ideals which have arisen from these conditions. A normal home, where there was human equality between mother and father, would have a better influence.

We must not overlook the effect of the proprietary family on the proprietor himself. He, too, has been held back somewhat by this reactionary force. In the process of becoming human we must learn to recognize justice, freedom, human rights; we must learn self-control and to think of others; have minds that grow and broaden rationally; we must learn the broad mutual interservice and unbounded joy of social intercourse and service. The petty despot of the man-made home is hindered in his humanness by too much manness.

For each man to have one whole woman to cook for and wait upon him is a poor education for democracy. The boy with a servile mother, the man with a servile wife, cannot reach the sense of equal rights we need today. Too constant consideration of the master's tastes makes the master selfish; and the assault upon his heart direct, or through that proverbial side-avenue, the stomach, which the dependent woman needs must make when she wants anything, is bad for the man, as well as for her.

We are slowly forming a nobler type of family; the union of two, based on love and recognized by law, maintained because of its happiness and use. We are even now approaching a tenderness and permanence of love, high pure enduring love; combined with the broad deep-rooted friendliness and comradeship of equals; which promises us more happiness in marriage than we have yet known. It will be good for all the parties concerned—man, woman, and child; and promote our general social progress admirably.

If it needs "a head" it will elect a chairman pro tem. Friendship does not need "a head." Love does not need "a head." Why should a family?

## Notes

1.  Chapter II, from *Our Androcentric Culture*, a work first published serially in *The Forerunner* (1909-1910) and subsequently as a book in 1911.
2.  *Monogamous*, a family type where there is only one husband married to one wife at any given time. *Polygamous*, the practice of having more than one wife or husband at the same time. *Polygyny* occurs when a man has more than one wife at the same time, and *polyandry* is a family type wherein a woman has more than one husband at the same time—this latter form is rare. For an accessible, contemporaneous discussion of family forms, see Elsie Clews Parsons, *The Family: An Ethnographical and Historical Outline with Descriptive Notes* (New York: G.P. Putnam's Sons, 1906).
3.  Honoré de Balzac (1799-1850), French novelist and playwright. The quote is more typically rendered as: "Woman's virtue is man's *greatest* invention." Note Gilman's alternate spelling.
4.  Edward Roland Sill (1841-1887) was an American poet.
5.  Gilman refers here to the practice of "foot-binding."
6.  An *odalisque* was a virgin female slave during the time of the Ottoman Empire.
7.  By *simiacrum*, Gilman presumably intends *similacrum*, an obsolete spelling of *simulacrum*. Thus, "something having merely the form or appearance of a certain thing, without possessing its substance or proper qualities" (*Oxford English Dictionary*).

# 2

# How Home Conditions
# React upon the Family (1909)

Discussion of social processes, to be fruitful, must rest on some hypothesis as to the nature and purpose of society. It is here assumed that society is a life-form in course of evolution, that its processes are to be measured like those of other life-forms, as they affect the three main issues of existence—being, reproduction, improvement.

In so far as social processes are genetic they interest us as students and critics; in so far as they are telic[1] they form the most practical and important subjects of study. The family has its origin in the genetic process of reproduction; but is modified continually by telic forces. In its present form it is an institution of confused values, based on vital necessity, but heavily encumbered with rudiments of earlier stages of development, some beneficent, some useless, some utterly mischievous; and showing also the thriving growth of new and admirable features.

We must consider it first on its biological basis, as a sex-related group for the purpose of rearing young; and the effect of conditions upon it should be measured primarily by this purpose.

Next we find in the existing family clear traces of that early long-dominant social unit, the woman-centered group of the matriarchate. Our universal and deep-seated reverence for the mother-governed home, with its peace, comfort, order, and goodwill, has survived many thousand years of patriarchal government, and refuses to be changed even by innumerable instances of discomfort, discord, waste, and unhappiness.

Superimposed upon this first social group comes the establishment of the patriarchate, the family with the male head, based upon the assumption by the male of sole efficiency as transmitter of life.[2] In this form the family enters upon an entirely new phase and includes purposes hitherto

11

unknown. It becomes a vehicle of masculine power and pride—was indeed for long their sole vehicle: it produces its ethics, its codes of honor, its series of religions, its line of political development through tribe and clan, princedom and monarchy, its legal system in which all personal and property rights are vested in the man, and its physical expression in the household of servile women. It is from this period that we derive our popular impressions that the family is the unit of the state, that the man is the head of the house, and other supposedly self-evident propositions. The patriarchal family, even in its present reduced and modified form, is the vital core and continuing cause of our androcentric culture.

Fourthly, we must view it as an industrial group of self-centered economic activities, the birthplace of arts and crafts as well as of persons. While the natural origin of these industries is in maternal energy, the voluntary efforts of the mother being the real source of human production, yet the family, as an economic group in the modern sense, is also an androcentric institution. Besides the mother's work for her children, the patriarchal family required the service of the man by his women—a claim which has no parallel in nature.

There is nothing in maternity, nothing in the natural relation of the sexes which should make the female the servant of the male. This form of economic relationship was developed when the man learned to take advantage of the industrial value of the woman and added to his profitable group as many women as possible. Moreover, when the masculine instinct of sex-combat swelled and broadened, blended with the hunter's predatory appetite, organized, and became war, then in course of time male captives were compelled to labor as the price of life, and set to work in the only social group then existent. It is to this custom, to this remote and painful period, that our institution owes its present name. Not father, mother, nor child, but servant, christens the family.

Further than this we find in our family group the development of a new relation, a new idea as yet but little understood, that which is vaguely expressed by the word marriage. Monogamy, the permanent union of one male and one female for reproductive purposes, is as natural a form of sex-relation as any other, common to many animals and birds, a resultant of continued and combined activities of both parents for the same end. This natural base of a true marriage should be carefully studied. Continued union in activity for a common purpose necessarily develops ease and pleasure in the relationship. The same couple can carry on these activities more easily than a new combination; hence monogamy.

In our human family we find many forms: androgyny,[3] polygyny, and then the slow and halting evolution of monogyny.[4] Monogynous marriage should include sex-attraction, romantic love, and a high degree of comradeship. It is now our common race ideal, recognized as best for the advantage of the child and the individual happiness of the parent; also, through greater personal efficiency, for the good of society. This form of marriage is slowly evolving in the family, but is by no means invariably present.

Lastly we must bear in mind that the family is our accepted basis of mere living; it, and its outward expression, the home, are so universally assumed to be the only natural form of existence, that to continue on earth outside of "a family," without "a home," is considered unnatural and almost immoral. In this regard the family must be studied as ministering to the health, comfort, happiness, and efficiency of adult individuals, quite aside from parental purposes, or those of marriage; as for instance in the position of adult sons and daughters, of aged persons no longer actively valuable as parents; or of co-adjacent aunts, uncles, and cousins; as also in relation to the purely individual interests of members of the family proper.

When we now take up our study of home conditions, we have definite ground from which to judge and measure them. How do they react upon the family in regard to those three major purposes of life—being, reproduction, improvement? Do they best maintain human life? Do they best minister to the reproduction of the species? And to the evolution of monogyny? Above all do they tend to race improvement?

Mere existence is no justification, else might we all remain Archaean rocks.[5] Reproduction is not sufficient, else the fertile bacterium would be our ideal. All social institutions must be measured as they tend not only to maintain and reproduce, but to improve humanity. We will make brief mention of our essential home conditions and examine their reaction on the family as touching: (a) marriage, (b) parentage, (c) child-culture, (d) the individual and social progress. What are our essential home conditions?

Here we are confronted with so vast and tumultuous a sea of facts; noisy, painful, prominent facts; that proper perspective is difficult to obtain. Here we are confronted also with the most sensitive, powerful, universal, and ancient group of emotions known to man. This complex of feelings, tangled and knotted by ages of ironbound association; fired with the quenchless vitality of the biological necessities on which they rest; intensified by all our conscious centuries of social history; hallowed, sanctified, made imperative by recurrent religions; enforced with cruel penalties by law, and crueller ones by custom; first established by those riotous absurdities of dawning ethics, the sex-taboos of the primitive savage, and growing as a cult down all our ages of literature and art; the emotions, sentiments, traditions, race-habits, and fixed ideas which center in the home and family—form the most formidable obstacle to clear thought and wise conclusion.

Forced by increasing instances of discontent, inefficiency, and protest within the group, we are beginning to make some study of domestic conditions; but so far this study has been on the one hand superficial; and on the other either starkly reactionary or merely rebellious.

The first home conditions forced upon our consideration are the material. Here we note most prominently the effects of economic pressure in our cities; the physical restriction of the home in the block, the tenement, the apartment house; the devastating effects of the sweatshop; the tendency toward what we call "cooperative" housekeeping.

As far as mere physical crowding is a home condition we may find that as far back as the cliff-dwellers, find it in every city of the world since there were cities, find it consistent with any form of marriage, with families matriarchal, patriarchal, polygynous, and monogamous. The Jew throughout Christian history has suffered from overcrowding as much as any people ever did; but he has preserved the family in a most intense form, with more success than many of the races which oppressed him. Even the sweatshop, while working evil to the individual, does but draw tighter the family bond.

Therefore, we are illogical in our fear of city-crowding as the enemy of the home, the destroyer of family life.

Others, identifying family life with the industries so long accompanying it, disapprove of that visible and rapid economic evolution in which the "domestic industries" as such dissolve and disappear. Yet if these observers would but study the history of economics they would find the period of undisputed "home industries" was not that of high development in family life, but rather of the mixed group of women slaves and male captives, when marriage in our sense was utterly unknown. The attempt to "revive home industries" is not difficult, since our modern family still maintains that primitive labor status; but it is reactionary, and tends to no real improvement.

"Cooperative housekeeping," as a term, needs brief but clear discussion. The movement to which the phrase is applied is a natural one, inevitable and advantageous. It consists in the orderly development of domestic industries into social ones; in the gradual substitution of the shirt you buy for the shirt your wife makes, of the bread of the public baker for the bread of the private cook, of the wine of known manufacture and vintage for the wine made for you by your affectionate great-aunt. All industry was once domestic. All industry is becoming social. That is the line of industrial evolution. Now what is "cooperative housekeeping?" It is an attempt to continue domestic industry without its natural base. The family was for long the only economic unit. The family is still, though, greatly reduced and wastefully inefficient, an economic unit. A group of families is not a unit at all. It has no structure, no function, no existence. Individuals may combine, do combine, should combine, must combine, to form social groups. Families are essentially uncombinable.

Vintner, brewer, baker, spinner, weaver, dyer, tallow-chandler, soap-maker, and all their congeners[6] were socially evolved from the practicers of inchoate domestic industries. Soon the cook and the cleaner will take place with these, as the launderer already has to a great degree. At no step of the process is there the faintest hint of "cooperative housekeeping." Forty families may patronize and maintain one bakeshop. They do not "cooperate" to do this; they separately patronize it. The same forty families might patronize and maintain one cookshop, and never know one another's names.

If the forty families endeavored to "cooperate" and start that bakeshop, or that cookshop, they would meet the same difficulty, the same failure, that always faces illegitimate and unnatural processes.

The material forms of home life, the character of its structure and functions depend upon the relation of the members of the family. In analyzing home conditions, therefore, we will classify them thus:

## A. Ownership of Women

It is to this condition that we may clearly trace the isolation of the home, the varying degree of segregation of the woman or women therein. The home is inaugurated immediately upon marriage, its nature, and situation depending upon the man, and in it the man secludes his wife. In this regard our home is a lineal descendant of the harem. It is but a short time since the proverb told us "the woman, the cat, and the chimney should never leave the house;" and again, "A woman should leave the house but three times—when she is married, when she is christened, when she is buried." In current comment upon modern home conditions, we still find deep displeasure that the woman is so much away from home. The continued presence of the woman in the home is held to be an essential condition. Following this comes—

## B. Woman-Service

The house is a place where the man has his meals cooked and served by the woman; his general cleaning and mending done by her; she is his servant. This condition accompanies marriage, be it observed, and precedes maternity. It has no relation whatever to motherhood. If there are no children, the woman remains the house-servant of the man. If she has many, their care must not prevent the service of his meals.

In America today, in one family out of sixteen, the man is able to hire other women to wait upon him; but his wife is merely raised to the position of a sort of "section-boss;" she still manages the service of the house for him. This woman-service has no relation to the family in any vital sense; it is a relic of the period of woman-slavery in the patriarchal time; it exhibits not the evolution of a true monogamy, but merely the ancient industrial polygamous group shorn down to one lingering female slave. Under this head of wife-service, we must place all the confused activities of the modern home. Reduced and simplified as these are, they still involve several undeveloped trades and their enforced practice by nearly all women keeps down the normal social tendency to special-ization. While all men, speaking generally, have specialized in some form of social activities, have become masons, smiths, farmers, sailors, carpenters, doctors, merchants, and the like; all women, speaking gen-erally, have remained at the low industrial level of domestic servants. The limitation is clear and sharp, and is held to be an essential, if not the essential, condition of home life; the woman, being married, must work in the home for the man. We are so absolutely accustomed to this rela-tion, that a statement of it produces no more result than if one solemnly announces that fire is hot and ice cold.

To visualize it let us reverse the position. Let us suppose that the conditions of home life required every man upon marriage to become his wife's butler, footman, coachman, cook; every man, all men, necessarily following the profession of domestic servants. This is an abhorrent, an incredible idea. So is the other. That an entire sex should be the domestic servants of the other sex is abhorrent and incredible.

Under this same head we may place all the prominent but little under-stood evils of the "servant question." The position is simple. The home must be served by women. If the wife is unable to perform the service other women must be engaged. These must not be married women, for no married man wishes his private servant to serve another man. When the coachman marries the cook, he prefers to segregate her in the rooms over the stables, to cook for him alone. Therefore our women servants form an endless procession of apprentices, untrained young persons learning of the housewife mainly her personal preferences and limitations. Therefore is the grade of household services necessarily and permanently low; and household service means most of the world's feeding, cleaning, and the care of children. The third essential home condition is:

## C. The Economic Dependence of Women

This is the natural corollary of the other two. If a man keeps a servant he must feed him, or her. The economic dependence of the woman follows upon her servitude. The family with the male head has assumed that the male shall serve society and the female shall serve him. This opens up an immense field of consequences, reacting most violently upon the family, among which we will select here two most typical and conspicuous. Suppose that the man's social service is of small value as we measure and reward our laborers. His return is small. His wages we will roughly estimate at $600 a year, a sum the purchasing power of which is variable. In our present conditions, $600 is little enough for one person. For two it allows but $300 each. For six, if they have four children, it is $100 a year apiece—less than $2.00 a week for each, to pay for food, clothes, shelter, everything. This visibly spells poverty. While one man's production is worth to society but so much, and while that one man's production is forced to meet the consumption of six; so long, even without any other cause, the resultant is general poverty—a persistent condition in the majority of homes. To segregate half the productive energy of the world and use it in private service of the crudest sort is economic waste. To force the low-grade man to maintain an entire family is to force a constant large supply of low-grade men.

The second of these consequences is the unnatural phenomenon of the idle woman. The man, whose sex-relation spurs him to industry, and whose exceptional powers meet special reward, then proceeds to shower gifts and pleasures upon the woman he loves. That man shall be "a good provider" is frankly held to be his end of the family duty, a most essential condition of home life. This result, as we so frequently and sadly see, is the development of a kind of woman who performs no industrial service, produces nothing, and consumes everything; and a kind of man who subordinates every social and moral claim to this widely accredited "first duty"; to provide, without limit, for his wife and children.

These two home conditions: the enormous tax upon the father, if he is poor, together with the heavy toil of the mother, and the opposite one of the rich man maintaining a beautiful parasite, have visible and serious results upon the family.

The supposedly essential basic relations, the ownership of woman, the servitude of woman, and the economic dependence of woman, with their resultants, give rise to the visible material conditions with which we are familiar. The predominant concerns of the kitchen and dining room, involving the entire service of the working housewife, rigidly measure the limitations of such families; while the added freedom of the woman whose housework is done vicariously seldom tends to a nobler life. Our insanitary households, our false and shallow taste, our low standard of knowledge in food values and nutrition, the various prosaic limitations within which we are born and reared are in the main traceable to the arrested development of the woman, owing to the above major conditions of home life.

Let us now show the reaction of the conditions above stated upon the family in modern society, in the order given, as they affect: (a) marriage, (b) maternity, (c) child-culture, (d) the individual and society.

We are much concerned in the smooth and rapid development of a higher type of marriage yet fail to see that our home conditions militate against such development. The effect of the modern home, even with its present degree of segregation of women, with its inadequate, confused, laborious industrial processes, and with its overwhelming expenses, is to postpone and often prevent marriage, to degrade marriage when accomplished through the servile and dependent position of the wife, and also to precipitate unwise and premature marriage on the part of young women because of their bitter dissatisfaction with the conditions of their previous home. This last gives an advantage in reproduction to the poorer types. The wiser woman, preferring the ills she has to those she foresees only too clearly, hesitates long, delays, often refuses altogether; not from an aversion to marriage, or to motherhood, but from a steadily growing objection to the position of a servant.

The man, seeing about him the fretful inefficiency of so many misplaced women, hearing *ad nauseam* the reiterant uniform complaints on "the servant question," knowing the weight of the increasing burden for which the man must "pay, pay, pay," waits longer and longer before he can "afford to marry;" with a resultant increase in immorality.

This paradoxical position must be faced fully and squarely. The industrial conditions of the modern home are such as to delay and often prevent marriage. Since "the home" is supposed to arise only from marriage, it looks as though the situation were frankly suicidal. So far, not seeing these things, we have merely followed our world-old habit of blaming the woman. She used to be content with these conditions we say—she ought to be now—back to nature! The woman refuses to go back, the home refuses to go forward, and marriage waits. The initial condition of ownership, even without service, reacts unfavorably upon the kind of marriage most desired. A woman slave is not a wife. The more absolutely the woman is her own mistress, in accepting her husband and in her life with him, the higher is the grade of love and companionship open to them. Again, the economic dependence of the woman militates against a true marriage, in that the element of economic profit degrades and commercializes love and so injures the family. It may be said that the family with the male head cannot exist in a pure form without its original concomitants of absolute personal ownership and exploitation of woman. When the ownership is no longer that of true slavery but enters the contract stage, when marriage becomes an economic relation, then indeed is it degraded. Polygyny is a low form of marriage; but, as modern polygynists have held, it at least tends to preclude prostitution. The higher marriage toward which we are tending requires a full-grown woman, no one's property or servant, self-supporting and proudly independent. Such marriage will find expression in a very different home.

Next comes the reaction upon motherhood, the most vital fact in the whole institution. Our home conditions affect motherhood injuriously in many ways. The ownership of the woman by the man has developed a false code of morals and manners, under which girls are not reared in understanding of the privileges, rights, and pre-eminent duties of motherhood. We make the duty to the man first, the duty to the child second—an artificial and mischievous relation. There is no more important personal function than motherhood, and every item of arrangement in the family, in the home, should subtend its overmastering interests.

Ownership of women first interferes with the power of selection so essential to right motherhood, and, second, enforces motherhood undesired—a grave physiological evil. The ensuant condition of female servitude is an injury in demanding labor incompatible with right maternity, and in lowering the average of heredity through the arrest of social development in the mother. It is not good for the race that the majority of its female parents should be unskilled laborers, plus a few unskilled idlers.

In poverty the overworked woman dreads maternity, and avoids it if she can. If she cannot, her unwelcome and too frequent children are not what is needed to build up our people. In wealth, the woman becomes a perpetual child, greedy and irresponsible, dreads maternity, and avoids it if she can. Her children are few and often frail. Neither the conditions of the poor home nor of the rich tend to a joyous and competent maternity.

In this one respect the home, under present conditions, is proven an unfit vehicle for the family. In itself, it tends to reduce the birthrate, or to lower the quality of the most numerous children; and all of them inherit the limitations of a servile or an irresponsible motherhood.

As regards child-culture, our home conditions present a further marked unfitness. Not one home in a thousand even attempts to make provision for child-culture. If the home has but one room that room is a kitchen; but few indeed are the families who can "afford a nursery." Child-care is wholly subordinate to kitchen service; the home is a complicated, inconsistent group of industries, in which the child must wait for spare moments of attention; which attention when given is that of a tired cook, or a worried housekeeper. No clearer comment can be made on the inadequacy of home conditions to serve their natural ends than in this major instance; they do not promote, but on the contrary, they prohibit the development of higher standards of child-culture.

As to mere maintenance of life, our children die most numerously during the years of infancy, when they are most wholly at home. As to reproduction, we have shown the effect on that; and as to improvement, it is a general admission that the improvement of the human stock does not keep pace with material progress. We need here a wise revision of domestic conditions in the interests of the child. At present any man who has a home to let, be it room, apartment, or house, prefers his tenants to be without children. The home, the birthplace, the rearing-place, is not built, fitted, nor managed for the benefit of children.

What is its further effect on the individual—and through him on society? Do the common home conditions of our time promote health, insure peace and comfort, tend to that higher development of the individual so essential to social progress?

Here we find another large ground for criticism. Modern society calls for individuals broad-minded, public-spirited, democratic, courageous, just, intelligent, educated, and specialized for social service. The family with the male head and its accompanying conditions of woman-ownership, service, and dependence tends to maintain in our growing democracy the grade of development, the habits of mind, the childish limitations of its remote past. In it is a masculine dominance which finds expression in our political androcracy. In it is a degraded womanhood which not only limits individual development in the mother, but checks it in the father through heredity and association, and acts powerfully to keep back the progress of the child. Because of the low grade of domestic industry, the food habits of humanity have remained so long what they are, tending to self-indulgence and excess, to extravagance, to many forms of disease.

Mere confinement to a house is in itself unwholesome, and when that house is a cookshop and laundry, it is further disadvantageous. The man, bound in honor (in his androcentric code of honor) to provide at all costs for his dependent family, has saddled himself with the task of making the product of one meet the consumption of many; and in making the woman a non-productive consumer, he has maintained in half the world the attitude of the child—the willingness to take, with no thought of giving an equivalent.

The social processes, left wholly to the male, are necessarily belligerent and competitive; and in the resultant turmoil, each man must needs strive to maintain his little island of personal comfort rather than to do his best work for the world.

Home conditions, which tend to results like these, require most serious consideration. They react upon the family in general as tending to restrict its natural evolution toward higher forms. They react upon it specifically as we leave seen, precipitating injudicious marriage, postponing marriage, degrading marriage; similarly do they affect motherhood, enforcing it where the woman is not free to choose, and where she is free to choose tending to postpone and prevent it because of its difficulties. The mechanical and industrial conditions of our homes, with their reaction upon character, lie at the base of that artificial restriction of motherhood so widely lamented.

Again they react upon child-culture, in age-long suppression of that greatest of sciences, in confining the care of little children to the ignorance of incompetent mothers and less competent servants. While the home enforces the condition of female servitude our children must continue to be born of and reared by servants.

Finally, these same conditions, these limitations in structure and function, this arrested womanhood and low-grade child-culture do not tend to develop the best individuals nor to promote social progress. Such as we are we are largely made by our homes, and surely we do not wish to remain such as we are. Our average health, longevity, efficiency, standard of comfort, happiness, and pleasure do not show the most wholesome influences.

The work of the constructive sociologist in this field is to establish what lines of change and development in our homes, what broad and hopeful new conditions, will act in harmony with social processes, will tend to a better marriage, a higher grade of motherhood, a freer and nobler environment for the individual. We need homes in which mother and father will be equally free and equally bound, both resting together in its shelter and privacy, both working together for its interests.

This requires structural and functional changes that shall eliminate the last of our domestic industries and leave a home that is no one's workshop.

The woman, no longer any man's property, nor any man's servant, must needs develop social usefulness, becoming more efficient, intelligent, experienced. Such women will bring to bear upon their proper problems, maternity and child-culture, a larger wisdom and a wider power than they now possess.

The home, planned, built, and maintained by men and women of this sort, would react upon its constituent family in wholly advantageous ways.

## Notes

1. "Telic," denoting the final end or purpose.
2. For a detailed and still reliable discussion of early family forms, see George Elliott Howard, *A History of Matrimonial Institutions* (Chicago: University of Chicago Press, 1904). Howard (1849-1928), a personal and professional acquaintance of Gilman, became president of the American Sociological Society (now the American Sociological Association) in 1917.
3. Gilman's referent here is unclear, and is likely a typographical error. *Androgyny* per se refers to a condition wherein individuals have both male and female traits—and this is nowhere considered a family type. She may have intended *polyandry*, the marriage of one woman to several unrelated men at the same time—where in its earliest form each of the men also had other unrelated wives. Or, she may have intended *androcracy*, wherein, as Lester F. Ward noted, "The primitive androcratic society was thus formed of patriarchal polygamous families and celibate men, the weaker of whom may have been also made slaves. All women were abject slaves, and the children were compelled to do any service of which they were capable" (*Pure Sociology*, New York: Macmillan, 1903: 352).
4. *Monogyny*, i.e., monogamy.
5. "Archaean," referring to the earliest geological time period.
6. "Congeners," in this instance, kindred or similar artisans.

# 3

# My Ancestors (1913)

I had been taught to revere my Ancestors, and did so. Ours was an Old Family. We had a Genealogical Tree, several Coats of Arms, and a Gallery of portraits.

There were also Books, Records, Rubbings, and a mass of documentary evidence as to the excellence and dignity of my Ancestors.

More immediately I had a Grandfather who was an Eminent jurist, and a Grand-Uncle who was a Major General. Back of that was a Great-Grandfather who was a Leading Divine, and one who was a Governor. Back of that I could enumerate many great names, Signers of the Declaration of Independence, Colonial Governors, and the like; and as soon as we crossed the ocean there were Lords and Ladies, Dukes and Earls, even Kings—in my Family Tree.

In the shadow of this tree I sat serene, firm in the determination never to do anything which should disgrace my Ancestors. As for myself, I was a Captain of Industry of no mean position, and furthermore was honored by an office in the administration of our legislative procedure. I belonged to all those Noble Societies which strive so hard, in our neglectful and irreverent age, to keep alive our veneration for our Ancestors, and subscribed my share to the funds which erected tablets and monuments to perpetuate the Glorious Deeds of the Past. Also I did my part politically, and I may say with modesty that it was not inconsiderable, to oppose those heady radicals who would shake the foundations of our prosperity and undermine the very basis of our national life by attacking that Marvelous Document, fruit of the best wisdom of our Ancestors—the Constitution of these United States.

Thus honorably and profitably engaged, as duteous almost as a Japanese, I was suddenly appalled by A Visitation. There came to me a Spirit in the night, who said:

"Wouldst thou see thine Ancestors? Yea or Nay?"

He towered above me, a Shadowy Huge Form, but my long descended courage was strong and I answered firmly, "Yea."

Then was I taken in the twinkling of an eye to an Immeasurable Plain, a Plain that seemed wider than the world. My vision, ranging across it, was marvelously magnified, so that I saw with piercing accuracy for mile on mile, yet found no limit. Neither did this Plain curve downward with the curving of the earth, but rather upward, on every side, like an Interminable Saucer.

I stood solitary, as one alone in the universe, and then suddenly, one on either side of me, appeared my father and my mother, vivid, alive, exactly as I remembered them. Beyond them my mother's father and mother stood beside her, and my father's father and mother behind him, also as I remembered them, save that they did not seem so old. Beyond these, following the same order stood my mother's mother's father and mother, my mother's father's father and mother, and my father's mother's father and mother, and my father's father's father and mother.

I will not try to enumerate the ring on ring of Ancestors which now encircled me. It was as though in concentric circles, neatly widening out like the blue ocean lines that follow the shore on the map, stood each generation of my Ancestors. In the first ring only my two parents; in the second ring my four grandparents; in the third my eight great-grandparents. In steady multiplication by two they ranged away into the distance, doubling in number in every circle, till in the twentieth row there stood one million, forty-eight thousand, five hundred and seventy-six ancestors. That must have been about the thirteenth century, I rapidly calculated. My intellect, like my eyesight, was abnormally clear. The distance, the terrible merciless distance, had neither softening mist nor diminishing perspective. With unstrained eye and unwearied mind I could see them all—and count them all.

It occurred to me also as the numbers grew, that these were only direct ancestors—that all the collaterals were left out. My brothers and sisters were absent, my uncles and aunts—of all this measureless array only one child of each couple was present—my own direct ancestor. Following this thought I suddenly lost the swelling sense of pride which had at first lifted my heart. It is true that these were all my own individual ancestors, but it was also true that I was by no means their only descendant.

Leaping backward in my illumined mind to that twentieth row of ancestors—they did not seem far back either, nor far off, physically—I hastily and unerringly computed their children—allowing them but two surviving offspring. By that allowance—and I groaned in spirit as I remembered the "large families" of the past—by that irreducible minimum I found that in the even line of twentieth cousinship I was but one descendant among 274,877,906,944. I had to share my ancestors with all the people of the earth, and then I saw that this was far more than the population of the earth, and remembered that their numbers had been mercifully reduced by frequent intermarriages.

Then did my parents speak to me saying: "Honor thy father and thy mother—as we did." And they passed me on to the next row.

My two parents were intimate and affectionate. My four grandparents were affectionate also. My eight great-grandparents looked at me with dim pride. But my sixteen great-great-grandparents did not know me from Adam. No one did, after that. I was passed on from row to row, with the same phrase: "Honor thy father and mother—as we did."

Each circle I walked around, looking first with affection, and then with interest and admiration, at my ancestors, recognizing many of them by their portraits. In the fourth row, however, I found several totally unfamiliar, and some I was forced to admit less desirable than others. One of these, a handsome woman enough, but evidently of lower birth and breeding, seemed to note my inner criticism.

"Honor thy father and mother," said she, "as I did." And at that I felt compelled to leave the pacing of concentric circles and to follow *her* father and mother up the line.

From this pursuit I returned, shamed to the soul, only to be seized on similarly by a fierce, coarse-faced ancestor in the fifth row, and made to trace *his* fathers and mothers to similar mortification.

It is true the Lords and Ladies, Dukes and Earls were here and there; also some Kings in the distance. The farther back the row the more frequently the Kings were found, each standing tall, in robe and crown. But those rings were also wider far, and side by side with Lord and King, in the same circle, equally my ancestors, I found strange company. In that great mass of human beings were every grade, not only Kings, but Slaves. Not only those proud pure Ladies in their ruffs and stomachers, but others not proud, not Ladies—not even pure.

Mixture of race, I found, scarce any in the world not represented. Yes, there was a Spanish ancestor, back of him a Moorish ancestor, back of her, with darkening skin and thickening lip—a Nubian line. In my veins ran the blood of Ethiopia! Strange cousins had I, Javanese and Jew, Russian, Mongolian—there was no limit to their range in race.

Nor in condition.

Nor in honor.

Then a Voice said: "Let the Kings stand alone!" And I looked over an empty waste and saw those few far-off Kings.

"Let the Slaves stand alone!"

And I looked, dreading, and first here one, and there one, thicker and thicker they stood, till in the far-off rows the serfs and slaves were almost all the throng.

"Let the Criminals stand alone!"

And they were many—many; thieves and pirates, murderers, courtesans, the cold-hearted tyrants and hired bravos of the past.

Then the Voice said: "Advance!"

And all those widening rows of ancestors came nearer, disappearing row by row as they approached. I knew the rough estimate of three generations to a century; I knew, as one knows many things one never thinks about, that our whole Christian era was covered by but sixty generations. I knew, or could have known had I ever counted, that the whole period of recorded history was a matter of only some hundred and fifty to three hundred generations. Ten thousand years, B.C., if we have lived that long, would only mean three hundred rings of ancestors.

Now I stood there watching these advancing lines, each coming forward and standing for awhile that I might observe them; each saying solemnly: "Honor thy father and mother—as we did!"

Such ancestors! Such wild barbarians from Northern Europe, such mysterious Asiatics, fierce-eyed Arabs, half-civilized Islanders.

In the same ring would stand side by side, equally related to me, a noble Roman with his rose-wreathed curls, and a sinewy Kaffir,[1] as proud of his "head ring" as the Roman of his wreath.

Long before we reached Rome the majority of my ancestors were clad in skins, and soon, as row on row came forward with their solemn cry, they were not clad at all. In those earlier lines there would be one or two richly garbed, some Egyptian, Chaldean,[2] or Mongolian, but all the others fur-clad savages or naked slaves.

I noticed with real surprise that the rings no longer widened, but narrowed. The more remote my ancestors, the less there were of them. The glories and honors, the gay garments and proud crowns, were all gone now, and I saw only dark, low-browed faces and bare, lean limbs. But each row, reaching back to the one behind it, said again: "Honor thy father and mother—as we did." And now the lean limbs were no longer bare, butshaggy, the low brows lower, the jaws more prominent, the noses flatter, the stature lower.

And they ceased speaking.

"No! No!" I cried in horror, as the nightmare ranks advanced. "Oh, stop them! Stop them!"

But they came.

Shorter, hairier, fiercer, more bestial, yet each row so like the one that preceded it none could dispute their close relation. On they came, halted and stood to gibber at me, and gave place to those behind.

And these stretched back so long!

My beaded fringe of modern dignitaries seemed but the merest edge on the border of civilization, that border narrowed momently in contrast to the long, dark web of life behind.

I shrieked aloud as I saw now, remote behind these furry shapes, the high-reared horrid heads of earlier things—shrieked and fell fainting.

\* \* \*

Then I was roused by the great Voice:

"Coward! Egoist! Short of sight and narrow of mind! Is it nothing to be One with the Whole World—the Child of Nature and the Child of God? If thou canst no longer honor thine ancestors, learn to honor, love and serve the human race, thy cousins, and the nobler men and women who are to come. Cease to worship at the Grave, and learn to look for God in men to come, not among buried bones."

### Notes

1.  Kaffir, originally a Muslim term referring to Black Africans who refused to accept Islam (Cf., *The Modern Eclectic Dictionary of the English Language*, 1904). Today, according to the *Oxford English Dictionary*, the word has become a general term of insult and opprobrium.
2.  Chaldean, a native of ancient Babylon or what is known today as Iraq.

# 4

# The Power of the Farm Wife (1915)

We speak of "the housewife" in universal admission that a woman marries not only a man, but a house. There are several million women in our country who are married not only to a man and a house, but also to a farm.[1]

In Agriculture, Forestry, and Animal Husbandry, the classification based on the census of 1910 shows 12,659,203, the great majority, being farmers.[2] Most of them are men and most of them are married—a farmer without a wife is almost as badly off as a missionary.

The huge "Bonanza" farms[3] of the West where the labor is transient and provided for in a sort of barrack system, may be run by bachelors, though even then mere loneliness may drive a man to marry, but the ordinary American farmer, tilling his own acres with the help of a "hired man" or two, not only needs the company of a wife, but her services.

He hires a man because his labor is productive, adding to the cash returns of the farm; but the woman he thinks he cannot afford to hire—so he marries her.

Say we have, in round numbers, ten million farmers and ten million farmers' wives. That is a large proportion of our (also round) hundred million. It is practically half the adult population. The condition of the farmer and his industrial advancement are now being carefully studied; and very lately, a questionnaire has been issued to the farm-wife, asking her how she liked it.

The Agricultural Department sent out 50,000 letters to Mrs. Farmer, but they received only a little over 2,000 replies—only one woman in twenty-five answered.[4] This in itself is a suggestive commentary. Were they too tired to take the trouble to write a letter on such a vital question? Were they too dull to see the importance of it? Did Mr. Farmer, when he went to the post-office, read that letter for Mrs. Farmer and think it better for her peace of mind—and his—not to raise the question of whether she was contented or not?

Some of those who answered were contented, a few enthusiastic. Many were discontented, and there was a pathetic agreement as to the grounds of discontent—loneliness and overwork. Even those who were content to work, and work hard, for their own families, objected to the extra work, and ignominy, of having to labor for and wait upon the hired men.

This is a custom accepted, as so many customs are, from mere usage; but if any man will try to reverse the position and see himself expected to fetch and carry for the hired girl, he will perhaps see a new light. To wait on his wife would be a novelty to some; though most American men are willing to; but to wait on his wife's servant—that would be another matter.

Yet, this is what the farmer's wife must do; losing her family privacy, admitting to her table these boarders, who are, to say the least, not an elevating influence.

The importance of the subject in our national life is most imperative. Not only is the business of agriculture the basis of our civilization, but the country life is, or ought to be, best for our children. If the women do not like it; if, as fast as they can, they seek to leave the farms and live in cities; this adds to the already pressing city problems, and tends to weaken the people by improper living conditions.

Children ought to grow up in the country, all of them. A city is no place to raise any kind of young animal—even the human. Yet at present the conditions of country life are by no means such as best to develop our little ones. Even in health, the country bred child does not stand as far ahead as he ought to. Worn-out mothers, tired, overworked, unhappy mothers, do not bear the best children, or rear them the best.

The farm-wife has not only her own health and happiness to consider; not only her influence on the country's greatest industry; but her duty to her children, to half the children of the country—some thirty million of them.

Almost anyone will admit the importance of this matter; and most people, who know the conditions, will admit that they are not what they should be. The practical question is: "What can we do about it?"

A farmer's wife may read this article thus far, and say: "That's all very well, but what can I do?" In answer to which the first thing is to rouse in each individual woman's heart a sense of the power of numbers, when united. This is not proposing an organization of ten million women over our three million square miles. That is quite too large an undertaking—for the present.

But we have now a Farmer's National Congress, representing more than three million men—why should not their wives be represented too?

Here is what the Farmer's congress urges: "General parcel post; liberal Federal aid for good roads and inland waterways; teaching of agriculture in the public schools; a Federal pure seed law; head tax and illiteracy test on immigration; a rural credit system not controlled by banking power; a law to prevent imitation of butter; legislation to curb water-power monopolies; National and State control of land fraud agencies; protection of co-operative enterprises." It opposes "ship subsidies; interstate liquor traffic into known dry territory; and free distribution of seeds."

All these show a large common interest among farmers (almost a third of them are organized), and a keen grasp of their needs and of measures to meet them. But it does not show the faintest recognition of that so-called "partner" at home, save, of course, as she benefits by the general improvement of the family.

Now suppose we had a Congress of three million Farmers' Wives. What could they "urge," and what "oppose?" They would doubtless add their votes—in the eleven free states[5]—to secure those general improvements; but how would they seek to benefit themselves and their children?

How about an "eight-hour law" for all women who are mothers? We are very keen in pointing out the injury to mothers of hard work outside the home for wages; why do we not see the injury of hard work inside the home without wages?

The farmer's wife works ten, twelve, fourteen hours a day. From five to eight is fifteen hours—and many a tired woman does not get the last dish wiped and put away, the last child in bed, before eight.

"The man works just as long," you say. Not quite. He stops at suppertime generally. Besides, even if it is for the same hours, he is not a mother. His strength may go altogether into his work; her's must go to building the bodies of her children, to furnishing them nourishment, and to the constant strain of their daily, and nightly, care. Let him do his work one day with a flock of little ones at his heels, and note the difference.

How about a recognized division of profits with the farm-wife?

When the year's work is done, both having labored their hardest, and a small surplus is on hand, whose is it?

When there is a question of a new mowing-machine or a new sewing-machine; a new cow-shed or a new cook stove; who is to decide?

Of course, on an economic basis, the farm machinery is measurably more important because with that the man earns the family living. If the woman was successfully running a dairy she would be entitled to her "separator" on the ground that it would "pay" to get one. She could show that in figures. How can she show the value of the new stove in figures? For that matter, how can she show her own value in figures? Has she any?

The common estimate of the value of a woman's working power is that of the old New England farmer who spoke of it as "Hen's time"—"Women's time is hen's time. Hen's time ain't no account." If one wife drops in the harness there are others to be had for the asking.

Now let the better educated modern woman look at this matter fairly and learn a new valuation of herself in figures. We will put it low, very low, merely at the rate of a "working housekeeper." She is certainly worth to her husband what he would have to pay any other woman *to do the same work*. This does not refer to her position as wife or as mother; these are not economic relations; or at least should not be; but to the value of her labor—the same labor that would be performed by a hired housekeeper. Her position is not merely that of a servant; if a servant was hired in her place the man would have to direct and oversee that servant, to take charge and order supplies. A working housekeeper has her room, her board, and her wages. These would vary, of course, in different communities; but $30 a month is a fair estimate; $360 a year. From this we will subtract $60 as the yearly cost of clothing the farmer's wife, leaving $300. That is not a large sum of money. Even with the clothes it is less than a dollar a day. Counting the board and lodging it might come up to $1.50 a day—the wages of a day laborer or a washwoman.

So, let every ordinary working farm-wife fix this fact in her mind; she is "worth," just for her labor, a room to herself, her board, $60 a year for clothes, and $300 besides.

Now our National Congress of three million Farmers' Wives, on that basis, would represent an annual income of nine hundred million dollars.

The Farmers would represent more, of course. The man must earn enough to feed the family, to meet the farm expenses, to pay the "help." That Congress of his stands for billions. The value of our farm products for 1914 is put at $9,751,119,000; which would average almost a thousand dollars a year to each farmer.

If out of this $300 were paid to the farm-wife for her share of the work, the family would have just as much money, but some of it would be hers—her own—to lay out as she thought best.

Very few men would be willing to do this. Even if they did it, they would feel that it was generous of them, a gift, a concession, not honestly earned. They pay the reapers, the thrashers, the fruit-pickers—whatsoever men they require; they pay, when so compelled, a "hired girl"; but to pay for the hard daily labor of the woman they marry is something difficult to think of as just. They would says: "But she is my *wife*; the whole thing belongs to Us—it's all done for Us, and the children."

The relation of wife does indeed confer its own dignity and its legal economic status. But the wife holds that place even if she does *no work at all*. The rich man's wife, though she may do nothing with her hands except have them manicured, is still a wife, entitled to all legal and economic privileges.

Parents are partners in their great work of raising up new people on earth; but men and women must realize that wife, mother, and housekeeper are three distinct relations.

Once thoroughly understanding this; with the sense of legitimate economic value—what more should our Congress of Farm-Wives do.?

They should begin to see the power of their position as mothers and the duty that goes with the power.

They should face the problem of how to improve the conditions of child life on the farm. Let the man put his share of the profits into improving his land, his machinery, his "stock"; let the woman put hers into improving the human race—life's highest duty.

Let the Farm-Wives' Congress, three million strong, pay in two dollars a year each—$6,000,000, half for the general association, half for the local branches. For every thousand women forming a country association there would be a thousand dollars for local use. They could meet often in small groups in one another's houses, and monthly, in the county seat, in larger numbers, to discuss and carry out measures for local improvement. The general body, holding its annual meeting in state after state, to allow of wide attendance, should spend its $3,000,000, after necessary convention expenses were allowed for, on a National Headquarters at Washington, a resident secretary and office force, and in securing the most careful research and experiment work in improving domestic rural conditions; with the preparation of authoritative reports, simple and clear, to be sent to all members.

When some new measure was thoroughly discussed and approved and the annual Congress decided to undertake it, the membership could put up another dollar each, another $3,000,000, and see it through.

Three dollars a year is only twenty-five cents a month; not a heavy tax, even for a farmer's wife.

Here are some of the things that might be done:

After a year of wide study of the special literature prepared by the congress as to "Home and Farm Industries for Women," a certain number of members might apply to Headquarters for an outfit for such industries.

Suppose a number desired to take up bee keeping; raising flowers or small fruit for sale; improved egg supply; preserving or pickling for the market; anyone of the things that may be done on farms as productive industries. Three million dollars would go a long way in supplying the initial outfit, special reading matter, and perhaps the visit of an expert to see the work well started; as well as in securing a market for the product. If five thousand women started such new activities, there would be $600.00 apiece for them.

Now that the parcel post brings house-wife and farm-wife into practical communication, it should be easy for the city consumers to send to the nearest local branch of the association and order direct.

It would be worth while, in all large cities, to have a F.-W.L.O.—Farm Wives' Local Office—with a full list of supplies obtainable, and samples as far as practicable.

All this is a perfectly natural and legitimate extension of women's work into wider social channels.

The knowledge of the best methods of instruction for children in the country should be carried far and wide among women. The voting power, the "influence," the money of the Association, could be used in no better way than by improving the rural school system, organizing kindergartens with "collect" automobiles;[6] starting playgrounds, and all such lines of improvement. Local, dramatic, musical, and other societies could be fostered. All manner of advantages both to child and mother, by no means excluding father, would accrue.

Now suppose the Association to grow large and strong; its membership encouraged by years of successful undertakings, and wiser by some failures. There will be a strong feeling of fellowship, of the union that is power, of real comradeship and mutual support. They might feel that in spite of all they had done they were still handicapped by their isolation; that do what they would, the living conditions on widely separated farms, were not conducive to economy or happiness. Then, after full and careful study, they might adopt such a resolution as this:

"Resolved: that for the best interests of children, of women, and of men also, it is essential for dwelling houses to be so grouped as to allow of free communication and association among the residents."

"That while the farm land may be widespread there is no reason why the houses of the farmers should not be grouped at one point; placed centrally in the area under cultivation."

"That we will devote our funds this year to the purchase and arrangement of such a Farm Center as will allow of the best agriculture with improved social and educational condition."

A competent and trustworthy committee is appointed; careful study made of the best locality, climate, and other advantages; and a large tract of land purchased. In its center is a park and playground, around which are grouped the houses of the residents, with a Village Hall, a School, a General Store, a Laundry, a Food Laboratory, and Science Bureau, as well as the inevitable Blacksmith's Shop and Post Office. Each house has its own lawn and garden, as pretty and convenient as modern science and art can compass; a single "plant" furnishing heat and light to all. Back of the houses a ring of garden land, with the "truck farms," orchards, small fruit beds and the like. Beyond that a wider ring of corn, wheat, or whatever was the main crop of the region; and widest of all the pasture range.[7]

Each individual "farm" would be shaped like a piece of pie—a rather elongated piece; the "first bite" being the house lot. Roads could be run between each two to the outskirts, and crossed by circular ones where needed. The men would have to go a little farther to their work, but the women and children would be near enough together for the best fruits of companionship, and the greatest economy of labor.

By organizing their household work, and so devoting more time to production, they could at once live easier lives and earn larger incomes, while the men could earn more and need to spend less.

Such a group could be started by a number of young couples, intelligent, progressive young people, such as our agricultural colleges are turning out every year; and that $3,000,000 fund could buy land, put up buildings, public and private, for a hundred families; with enough for running expenses till the little village was well under way. And the Association would get all the money back from the residents, too, as they bought their farms and houses in yearly installments.

## Notes

1. The continuing struggles of farm women are well documented by Deborah Fink, *Agrarian Women: Wives and Mothers in Rural Nebraska, 1880-1940* (Chapel Hill, NC: University of North Carolina Press, 1992). More recent hardships are depicted in the searching 1998 PBS documentary film by David Sutherland, *The Farmer's Wife* (for details, see the film's website: www.pbs.org/wgbh/pages/frontline/shows/farmerswife/).

2. By the year 2000, farming, fishing, and forestry, as an occupation, claimed only 951,915 workers, a mere 7 percent of the American workforce (Census 2000 Briefs and Special Reports. Retrieved January 15, 2009 from www.census.gov/population/www/cen2000/html).

3. For a detailed study, see Hiram M. Drache, *The Day of the Bonanza: A History of Bonanza Farming in the Red River Valley of the North* (Fargo, ND: North Dakota Institute for Regional Studies, 1964).

4. The letters were mailed on October 1, 1913, by the US. Secretary of Agriculture. For verbatim replies, see U.S. Department of Agriculture, *Social and Labor Needs of Farm Women* (1915, Report No. 103), *Domestic Needs of Farm Women* (1915, Report No. 104), *Educational Needs of Farm Women* (1915, Report No. 105), and *Economic Needs of Farm Women* (1915, Report No. 106).

5. I.e., the eleven states that by 1915 had formally endorsed a woman's right to vote. Women in the USA did not enjoy universal suffrage until 1920, following ratification of the Nineteenth Amendment to the US Constitution.

6. "Collect" automobiles, i.e., transport cars to "collect" the children and take them to and from school.

7. Compare this land-use proposal with like-minded depictions of land utilization in Gilman's 1915 novel, *Herland*.

# Part II

# Men and Marriage

# 5

# Does a Man Support His Wife? (1911)

This special problem in socioeconomic relation is one which looks delusively simple, as being so universally before our eyes, and of such unbroken historic continuity; but it is in fact complicated most confusingly.[1]

We have first the complication of sex, causing us to judge an economic relation between a man and a woman as we would never judge the same relation between two men or between two women.

Second, we have the complication of different stages of economic development going on together in the same period.

Third, we have the complication of service performed and not paid for.

And fourth, we have the complication of that uncertain question as to how much "service" is of economic value.

In a large sociological sense no civilized human being is "self-supporting." We are all interdependent; living not by virtue of our own exertions, but by virtue of the exertions of many other persons; those before us and those beside us, whose combined labors make up human life.

In an individual sense a man may be called "self-supporting" who contributes to the world more in labor value than he takes out. If it costs other persons three hundred dollars worth of food, clothing, and shelter to keep a man alive, he must give three hundred dollars worth of labor to be "self-supporting." If it costs other persons three thousand or three million dollars worth a year to maintain a man, he must give that amount in labor to be "self-supporting."

If, in a lifetime, one puts into the world more than one takes out, there need be no sense of obligation. Yet our economic ideas are so confused that we speak of a man who lives on inherited money doing absolutely no productive work, and consuming all he possibly can, as being "independent"; and on the other hand consider those whose generous, ill-paid labor we live from day to day, as "dependents," to whom we have to "furnish employment."

Viewed from this side the life-long labors of the average married woman certainly should be considered as more than equal to all she receives in life, and, in that single sense, she may be academically considered as "self-supporting."

This is, however, but a metaphysical satisfaction; and in no way alters the glaring fact that the income of a married woman is by no means relative to her own economic exertions; but (a), to her husband's economic exertions, and (b), to his good pleasure.

Metaphysically she may solace her soul with the thought that her services are of sufficient value to entitle her to a large salary. Actually, her salary, wage, or income, even if guaranteed to her by law, could be no more than what was left of her husband's income after the household was provided for, even if he kept none at all! If he kept half, as the most modest of men might feel was right, there is the measure of her "support;" board wages, mere food, shelter, and warmth, as we must give even to draught animals, or slaves; and beyond that half of the surplus, if there is any.

If the husband's economic efforts are valuable, the wife's "support" improves. If they are of a low value, so is her "support." What she gets out of life is not proportioned to her labors, but to his.

In this painfully practical view the wife *is* supported by her husband. He must give to other persons enough labor to receive a return of food, shelter, and clothing for the family. If his powers are great, and he finds a market for them, he can "support" the family well. If his powers are small, or find no market, he cannot. If he is altogether unable to work, or is dead, the woman must learn to work for other persons in order to "support" the family.

Put it vividly in a single case.

Here is Mrs. Jones, working industriously all day in her house. She sweeps and dusts, scrubs and scours, washes and irons, cooks and clears away, sews, mends, makes beds, for twelve hours a day.

Her husband meanwhile works in a mill for ten hours a day and brings home as an equivalent of his labors, money, which means rent, coals, food, clothes.

She works as long as he, and at more intricate tasks, and does not feel that he "supports" her.

Now Mr. Jones dies. She remains in the home and goes on as before, performing those intricate tasks.

Then comes the rent bill, the coal bill, the bread bill, the meat bill—all the bills. Her labors are no equivalent. No one will give her a house, a fire, clothing, and food, for doing housework for herself—or for her children; and she has lost her former employer.

This is the actual economic position of a working housewife. She is a servant, on board wages. If her husband is so poor that he cannot afford to even feed a servant, then she has to work for other people—support herself—perhaps support him!

We may now change our question a little and say, "Does a man support his servant?"

Here is Mr. Smith, who earns enough to enable him to keep a "man." The "man" toils incessantly for his master. He is industry and care personified. He labors and thinks and devotes his life to the service of his master. He certainly earns his wages. But if his master grows too poor to pay those wages, too poor even to pay for food for two, then must the "man" find another employer; his first one can no longer "keep," *i.e.*, "support" a servant.

This shows that a human being may labor steadily and yet be "supported" at the same time. To support another person does not imply that the other person does not deserve it, has not earned it; but it does imply that the supporter is the employer, and that the employer depends on him.

This is the position of the married woman; she is privately employed by her husband, at house service.

Let us distinguish carefully between this, their economic relation, and their physiological, legal, emotional, or other relations. She is his wedded wife, and entitled by law, arbitrarily, to "support," even if she is sick and can do no work. She is his mate; they are co-partners in parentage.

They love each other, much or little as the case may be. They have mutual affection, respect, esteem; the pleasantness or unpleasantness of long habituation between them. All these have nothing whatever to do with their economic relation.

Industrially considered she is his housekeeper, or house-servant, on board wages.

Mrs. Pethick Lawrence speaks[2] of these unpaid labors of the housewife in the highest terms; not only as noble and beautiful in themselves, but as "a gigantic saving of the wealth both of the employer and the state."

She seeks to establish a higher claim for the dignity and honor of the housewife's position and for its economic value in particular.

This theory, while bravely and clearly set forth, is not only untenable, but of the gravest injury to the very cause it champions. What women need is not to be soothed and kept content in their economic position by any sweeping claims of its world-value, but to learn once and for all that their position is one injurious and degrading, not only to themselves, but to the world.

It may be safely said that as long as women, who constitute half the world, are content to live as private servants to the other half, our civilization must remain arrested and incongruous as we see it now.

A later culture, accustomed to the economic equality of men and women, will find it difficult to understand the peculiar anchylosis[3] of ideas which has for so long maintained this paradoxical position.

That the basic reverence of the male for the female has survived at all, through these ages of servile womanhood; that any legal justice has been accorded to a universally servile class; that a social equality even as superficial as ours can be maintained; these anomalies are proofs of the strength of biological and sociological forces, as against temporary artificial conditions.

The early relation of men and women, wherein the father hunted, and the mother carried, skinned, and cooked the game, was a fair enough partnership. The later stage, as among the Pueblos of our own Southwest, where the men own the fields and the women the houses, is a fair enough partnership. But since manufacture and exchange began, the whole range of progress, world progress, has been in the hands of men; and all its splendid rewards have been theirs.

The economic status of a nation lies in its "land and labor"; in its natural resources, and the quantity and quality of intelligence applied to them. As that intelligence grows, as new arts, new sciences, new inventions, are given to the world, the world grows rich and strong. Economic progress lies in the long path between that savage, hunting for himself and his family, and the present international distribution of the world's goods.

Here is where the economic position of woman is so misunderstood, for lack of sociological knowledge. Evidently the present visible woman is here, in the same century with the automobile, the air-ship, the International Postal Union. Yet her economic status is that of the squaw. She stays at home and cooks. She has the advantages of utensils and supplies developed by advancing civilization, but her *status*, in regard to getting a living, is just what it was then. He gets it—she cooks it.

When they began they were even. He got it, alone. She cooked it, alone.

Now he gets it by the highly developed complex interchange of specialized, organized modern industry. She still cooks it, alone.

This labor is honestly believed to be a saving; to the family and to the state.

It is not a saving; it is an unbearable expense.

The least efficient, most wasteful labor, is that of every man for himself. The next lowest is that of every woman for her man. Every man, to the poorest, thinks he must have one whole woman to cook for him; and they both think it is "economical"!

If they were not women, these innumerable cooks, this fifty per cent of the human race deliberately set aside to cook for the other fifty, no sane economist could bear the thought of such a colossal waste of labor.

If each man did for himself the work he expects of his woman, there would be no wealth in the world; only millions and millions of poor tired men, sweeping, dusting, scrubbing, cleaning, serving, mending, cooking, washing, ironing—and dying, for lack of food.

Fine words butter no parsnips—neither does housework. Some one has to raise the parsnips.

Suppose there were no women in the world. Would each man think he must have a whole other man to cook for him? Would the other man do it—on board and wages, so reducing the wealth of the world by half—and getting very little of that?

Men have passed that stage of labor, in civilized countries. Some of them, it is true, are still servants; but neither they nor anyone else have any delusions as to their work being a saving, either to the family which can afford to "keep a man," or to the state.

The question of how much personal service is of economic value may be clearly answered: as much as increases the economic value of the person served.

Consider first the case of one person, waiting on himself. His income depends wholly on the amount of time, strength, and intelligence he puts into productive labor. The amount of time, strength, and intelligence he can afford to spend on the setting of tables, the blacking of boots and mending of clothes, the making of cakes and pies, and ironing of table linen for himself, must be measured by its effect on his productive labor. Let us suppose that one hour a day spent in cooking is absolutely necessary to him, leaving nine for his productive labor.

If spending two hours a day in housework enables him to earn as much, or more, in the remaining eight, then he can afford that. If spending three hours a day in housework enables him to earn as much or more in the remaining seven, then he can afford that. But it can be readily seen that if he spent all his time doing housework for himself he would have nothing to eat; and that the limit of justifiable expense for him, in the time devoted to housework, is the amount absolutely necessary to maintain his best efficiency.

Then consider the case of a group of men working together on one economic base; as fifty lumbermen in a forest. Their economic product is cut wood: their income depends on how much wood they cut. If each man works ten hours a day, and his labor is worth ten cents an hour, this would represent a dollar a day for each, fifty dollars a day for the group, and one hour's labor of the group is worth five dollars.

Now, suppose each of these fifty men makes a fire, three times a day, and cooks his own meals, allowing for this two hours' time. This would equal ten dollars a day, sixty dollars a week, paid for service. Each man earns but one dollar a day, yet they are paying, collectively, ten for their cooking; to say nothing of the waste of the fifty fires and the fifty sets of cooking utensils. No set of men, working collectively, would be so foolish.

Neither do they settle the matter by dividing themselves into two economic classes, the one twenty-five cutting wood and the other twenty-five devoting all their time to cooking for and otherwise serving the woodcutters. If this were done there would be twenty-five men earning a dollar a day, and each paying that dollar to his cook—in which case he would have nothing, and the cook would have to buy the food out of his wages.

If the twenty-five woodcutters devised the brilliant idea of not paying the twenty-five cooks, and the twenty-five cooks, for some mysterious reason, acquiesced, there would still be but twenty-five dollars a day earned, where there had been fifty, and just as many persons to feed as before. The expenses of running that lumber camp would remain the same; the income would be reduced by half.

The twenty-five cooks might conceivably suppose that they were doing a service to the twenty-five woodcutters; might solace themselves for their lack of wages by imagining how much their services were worth; might add all manner of profuse attention to the really necessary cooking; might sit up all night to frost cake and whip syllabubs[4]—thus endearing themselves to their employers: but the painful economic fact remains that half the labor of that group was wasted.

"No, not half. Somebody has to cook!" protests the woodcutter, swinging his axe proudly; "you don't expect *me* to do it, I hope."

Yes, somebody has to cook. It is very bad economics for each one to do it himself—that cost ten dollars a day. The twenty-five cooks would cost twenty-five dollars a day if they were paid; but as they are not paid, the deluded woodcutters think the cost nothing.

What they cost is the money they do not earn.

And who should do the cooking?

As many cooks as are necessary to do the cooking for fifty men. One can do it, having nothing else to do. If our woodcutters were a little luxurious, and willing to pay, they might have two. Two, at a dollar a day, like the others.

Now we have forty-eight at productive labor, and two at what we might call conducive labor, indirectly productive; and no waste.

The expense of feeding the fifty would be alike, whether they all cut wood or all cooked. As a mere question of economics, for half the world to abstain from productive industry and become servants to the other half, is a waste of nearly 50% of human efficiency.

Then arises the question of sex, which is the main element of confusion in the case. The social value to the world of rearing human beings, and the psychic value to the husband of the affection of his wife, together with other "values" which need not be obtrusively mentioned, are confused with economic values, naturally enough.

To clear up this confusion, let us now treat of women alone, as we have been treating of men.

Let us suppose one woman, Mary Smith, self-supporting, a dress-maker. Her economic outfit consists of skilled labor. She manufactures garments for purchasers. They pay her for the garments.

She lives alone, "does" for herself, and earns two dollars a day.

Now this woman marries; her husband promptly dies, and she has posthumous twins. She now in due course "bears the long strain and sharp ordeal of childbirth, and becomes the sole minister to the manifold needs of her infant children." I quote from the article under discussion.[5]

What is the effect of this experience on her economic position?

She must still live. As she does not raise food, she must buy it. She must give labor to others that they may give food to her. This she does by dress-making as before. But now some of her energy has gone into bearing the children; some energy and some time must go into caring for the children: her economic output is decreased by that much.

It is no use asking the children to pay, though many parents literally do this—in later years; and we cannot sell the children nowadays; they are not marketable commodities.

Motherhood is not an economic function. It is physiological, but it is not economically productive. On the contrary, it is economically expensive.

While the children are under the age when they can rightly produce, they merely consume. To provide for them, more must be earned.

This woman, alone, would not expect to see her income raised because she was a mother. Her income depends on how many dresses she makes; not on how many children she has. Let us suppose that she gives half her time to the care of her children and the home, five hours a day. In this case she would earn one dollar a day instead of two, and have three to maintain on that sum.

Now appears Jane Jones, forewoman in a large shop, also earning two dollars a day, and conceives a violent affection for Mary. Moved by this affection, which is reciprocated, they become close friends. Then Jane says to Mary, "I have to pay half my money for board and lodging; why not pay it to you?" Then we can live together in peace and amity, and you will be the richer, while I am no poorer."

This is agreed upon. To give room and board and service to this friend does not take all the money she pays, and does not add materially to the hours spent in housework. The arrangement is a profitable one to Mary, and no new expense to Jane. Mary's income is again two dollars a day, twelve dollars a week, to feed and shelter four, while the beneficent Jane still has six dollars a week to spend on her own clothing and pleasure.

Now comes the great change; the change from a dignified, workable economic arrangement to that now commonly held by women. Jane becomes so ardent in her affection for Mary that she says, "Wilt thou be mine?"

"Why, I am yours," says Mary; "I love you dearly."

"Yes, but I cannot bear to think of your working at dressmaking for strangers! Give it up and work for me! All I have is yours! I will take care of you!"

Mary, under some delusion of greater respectability and deeper affection, rapturously accepts the proposition, and becomes Jane's.

Jane's what?

Jane's housekeeper and servant. Jane is delighted. Mary has more time to make fancy dishes for her, and to decorate the house, Jane's house. It is Jane's house because she pays the rent.

Her salary has not been raised. Out of her twelve dollars she has to pay all that Mary paid from hers—which has disappeared. Now, Jane must have car-fares, clothes, lunch, and tobacco, to say nothing of a little beer;

and these leave her less than twelve dollars for their combined expenses. They meet this loss with equanimity, for are they not "together"?

As a matter of fact they are no more together than they were before, but Jane prefers it. Jane likes to think that Mary is "hers" and works only for her. She likes to think that the house is "hers" and not Mary's. She did not like to board in Mary's house; she prefers to support Mary. And she does support her; very poorly, to be sure, but every bit that Mary eats, drinks, wears, in any way consumes, is paid for out of Jane's wages.

Jane is much poorer, of course, but bears it nobly—is she not sacrificing herself to support Mary?

And Mary, poor dear, is quite happy; for she loves Jane, and loves her children, and works from morning to night to care for and please them.

But can she claim that her position is a saving to anybody?

An economic relation is the same, whether between two men, two women, or a man and a woman. Women should not delude themselves with the idea that because they work so hard they are therefore in some mysterious way producing wealth, or even saving it.

They should learn that their economic position is one of gross waste; as that of the twenty-five cooks for the twenty-five woodcutters. Waste of time, waste of strength, waste of fuel, waste of utensils, waste of houseroom, waste of food; all this added to the enormous loss of what they might have produced. Not only is this a heavy loss in our economic wealth, but the preservation of this primitive status of labor in a world otherwise industrially advanced is a grave social injury.

It is the largest deterrent to the social evolution of women, tending to keep them over-personal and narrow-minded; and has a reactionary influence on the men, so lapped in personal service; and on the children who are reared in the atmosphere of servile womanhood.

The value of motherhood to the state is quite another matter, and so is the relation of the state to its young citizens. Whatever arrangements are made about that should be made by free women, in congress assembled. It is their affair.

But the whole difficulty lies in that one small phrase of the grasping male—"Wilt thou be mine?"

Why should she be "His?"

Mutual love, legalized marriage, happy parenthood; these are worlds removed from this last dragging remnant ancient savagery, the squaw-status, the slave status, of women.

Is not legal possession with enforced labor and no pay slavery?

And is slave labor economically advantageous?

When women are wise enough to be free, and free enough to be wise, they will learn to dissociate the joys of love, the status of marriage, the blessings and cares of motherhood, from the plain trade of cooking, and the labors of personal service.

## Notes

1.   This edition omits three introductory paragraphs.
2.   Emmeline Pethick Lawrence (1867-1954) was an English suffragist and co-editor (with her husband) of the journal, *Votes for Women*. The item Gilman references here was the lead article for the 21 July 1911 issue of *Votes for Women*.
3.   "Anchylosis," or stiffening.
4.   "Syllabubs," a dish made by mixing wine or cider with cream or milk, and thereby creating a soft curd.
5.   E.P. Lawrence, *supra*.

# 6

# Names—Especially Women's (1911)

Visiting one of our state legislatures, I heard the Clerk of the House gabble droningly off the names of the Senators assembled.

It was a large state, a large senate, a large list of names.

He reached the Smiths and recited them. "Smith, Albert A., Smith, Andrew R., Smith, Brandon P., Smith, Edward W.," till he came to John. Then it was "Smith, John D., Smith, John H., Smith, John J.;" and all those eminent officials had to distinguish them one from another in their names was the D. and the H. and the J.—mere initial letters, like so many handkerchiefs.

A name is meant to distinguish, and if possible to indicate distinction.

The onomatopoetic tendency, which gave us "water," "rumble," "murmur," "crash," "bang," and many others, shows the natural wish to have the word which indicates something express something of the character of the thing indicated. In sound as well as in sense we follow this line in the difference between the names of men and women, trying to express strength in the former, beauty, and grace in the latter. We have tried, in the old days when we did try to mean something with our naming, to call our girls after jewels, flowers, and the softer virtues.

Perhaps the latest effort to give meaning to names was among our Puritan ancestors, who not only called their sons Amminadab[1] and Eleazar,[2] but Steadfast, Goodfight, and Praise-the-Lord; while Patience, Prudence, Diligence, Forbearance, Faith, Hope, and Charity showed the characteristics they approved in women.

Different nations have different customs in the bestowal of names, both in their number, character and continuance; some having a rich and varied supply, others but a single cognomen.[3] It is told of a Spanish nobleman, visiting America, and inwardly displeased at the rudeness of a telegraph clerk, that he asked with soft courtesy, "And do you charge also for the signature?" When the clerk sneeringly answered, "No!" he presented his message signed with a score or so sonorous long-linked Spanish names, all honestly his own.

The Spanish method is indicative of long lines of blended ancestry; of much personal dignity and endless time.

"John D." or "John L." are shorter, and in some instances seem to carry enough distinction.

Two crippling influences have been at work to check the growth of names among us; the unimaginative imitative docility of many people, and the androcentric desire to repeat the name of the father. This is far less commonly observed in the names of mothers. Mary is not so anxious to see a little Mary running to her call, but John goes proudly on in John Jr., which is still more delightedly applied to John 3rd. Our names show the marks of this paternal prepotence in marked degree.

It has been shown that when sirnames[4] began to be added to the "christened" name, there were developed five general classes; first, the mere repeating of a name, as in Patrick Henry, or Henry George; second, the badge of fatherhood, as Johnson, Peterson, Robertson, and all that large assortment; third, the trade of the person to be indicated; as Carpenter, Baker, Butcher, Wright, Farmer, Shepherd, to the innumerable and omnipresent Smiths; fourth, the names of places: more dignified, these, as showing possession of property, or at least long association with it, as in Meadows, Hill, River, Fountain, Wells, Woods, Forest, with the long list of Westcotes, Eastcotes, Southcotes, Northcotes, and many more; and fifth, names based on some personal distinction; all the color names, as Black, White, Gray, Green; with Long, Short, Stout, and those like them.

Perhaps the latest wholesale adoption of sirnames was when the Jews of Germany were compelled by law to take to themselves names other than their tribal ones. It was difficult to prosecute, no doubt, among hundreds of Solomon Solomons. They seem to have been limited, too, to certain classes of natural objects, judging by all the Rose-trees, Lily-trees, Green-trees, High-trees; all the Rose-mountains, Green-mountains, and High-mountains; all the Fine-golds and Fine-silvers; the Gold-stones, Silver-stones, Ruby-stones, and Diamond-stones among them.

But whatever the sirnames may be, however derived, women have none of them. Few people seem to realize this. Since sirnames descend in the male line only; since boy as well as girl must wear their father's name; it never occurs to the girl, or to any one else, that she and her thousand mothers have never had the distinction of a sirname, beyond the badge of paternity.

In Iceland you may find "Johannisdottir" as well as "Johannissen"; but how about some Janeson, Maryson, Elizabethson?—to say nothing of Jane's or Mary's daughter?

This is but one of the many invidious distinctions between men and women under an androcentric culture. Men, being persons, had names. They must be distinguished from one another. Women, being female belongings, needed no badge save that of the man to whom they belonged. When they left their father's possession, when he gave this woman to be married to this man, she took the name of her new owner, naturally.

Years and years ago I wrote a little article entitled "The Women of John Smith," which appeared in that clever paper *Kate Field's Washington*.[5] Some of its points are here quoted.

It showed that the title "Mrs.," which is short for Mistress, indicates merely that the person bearing it is the wife of the real owner of the sirname following. Well, what of that? The woman remarks with a happy smile that she is proud to bear her husband's name. The man as proudly "gives her his name" when he marries her. He never thinks that in giving her his, he takes away hers—such as she had. She never thinks that she never really has any; that all that distinguishes one woman from another is which man she is the daughter of, or the wife of.

As a matter of fact, in previous history, this was all that mattered; as the woman had no social relations in life—merely their personal one.

They were somebody's daughters, and then somebody's wives; and were not anything else. Therefore they never felt, much less resented, their namelessness.

While property was in male hands; while inheritance was in the male line; while women had no functions other than those of females and private servants; such a condition passed unnoticed.

Now that women are coming into human relation, developing human characteristics, being known not merely as female relatives, but as personal and social relatives, they need names for the same reason that men need them. To this need they are slowly awakening.

When a woman has built up a business or established a professional reputation as Mary Smith, it is a serious pecuniary disadvantage to become Mrs. Peter Saunders, precisely as it would be a disadvantage to a man to have to change his name. This is recognized among men, and they preserve a "trade name," though every man of the original firm be out of it.

Some business women do this, remaining Mary Smith to the trade, but introduced socially, with modest pride, as Mrs. Peter Saunders.

So arbitrary are our ideas of what is honorable that the essential ignominy of losing one's name is mysteriously transmuted into an honor by long custom. Matrimony being an honorable estate, the only honorable one open to women, all its concomitants become, by association, honorable. When, as among the old Japanese or Jews, the wife was required to undergo personal defacement, shaving her head or removing her eyebrows, even this was accepted as a dignity. Was it not proof that the shaven one was married? And what more could be desired?

Let us dispassionately consider the kind of persons that are required to give up their names.

Those who inherit money with that condition attached; monks and nuns when they renounce the world and enter the monastery or convent; convicts when they too are shaven and go to prison; and women when they marry.

Is not the company suggestive?

Suppose you had a girl friend, born and reared in a certain city—one Nellie Satterlee—and you had left that city for some years, during which she had married. You come back and wish to find her. If you cannot remember her husband's name you cannot find her at all. Perhaps you do remember that she married a man named Roberts. You look up the Robertses, half a column of them. You think that his name was Henry. There are eight H.-something Robertses. You may now pay eight separate nickels to call up eight separate places, and inquire for the maiden name of the lady of the house! The servant does not know it. Her mistress, being interrogated, is annoyed. It does seem an impertinence from a stranger, and you are a stranger to seven of these Mrs. H. Robertses.

But if you want to find her brother, Billy Satterlee, there he is in the list, his name unchanged, whether he be a bachelor or three times married. A single woman, or a widow, appears in the city directory. A married woman does not.

Why this difference? Why this inconvenience and real loss, for women only?

If it be suggested that women should have permanent names of their own the usual reply is twofold; first, that we should not know whether they were married or not; second, that it would make trouble in the inheritance of property.

As to this last, the answer is that it would make far less trouble than now exists. Millions of dollars are lost to those who should inherit them by the fact that the inheritor's right came through the mother, *and could not be traced*. Millions more are wasted in laboriously tracing out their "female line" of descent; the whole difficulty lying in the fact that the female line is nameless.

As to knowing whether a woman is married or not—why should you?

You do not know whether a man is married or not, either by his name or by a glittering official ring. Again, why should you?

If one of the two needs to be so labelled, it should rather be the man; for he, masquerading as single, can commit bigamy and other serious offenses.

"It is a protection to her" some say.

Protection against what? Is it something like a collar on a dog, the license tag and name of master, showing that if you injure the animal you may have to answer for it?

In days of slavery, either in our own country or in the old feudal system, a "masterless man" was open to anybody's exploiting. So, it seems to be felt, is a masterless woman.

Suppose you are at a party. You sit talking with old friends, and see a fine woman approaching.

"Who is that?" you say; and your friends tell you "It is Ellen Fullerton."

"Is she married?"

"Yes—and has three children."

"Who was she?" (note the past tense!)

"She was a Pyecroft—don't you know?—the Kingston Pyecrofts; related to the Hammersleys"—and so on and so on—if they happen to know.

But suppose they do not happen to know? What of that. You may either pursue a close personal acquaintance with Ellen Fullerton and find out, or let it alone. There is no reason why you should have your curiosity gratified as to her personal relations—unless, indeed, you want to marry her. Time enough then to find out.

One is introduced as "Susan Mortimer." One's interlocutor presently inquires "Miss or Mrs.?" One is tempted to inquire "What it that to you Sir?"

He was introduced as Paul Waterson. You did not instantly demand of him "Are you a bachelor or married?"

## Notes

1. Amminadab, the father of Nashon, leader of the tribe of Judah (see *Numbers* 1:7, 2:3).
2. Eleazar, the key figure through whom tradition traced the line of priestly descent from Aaron (see *Josuah* 24:33).
3. "Cognomen," or surname.
4. The preferred spelling today is "surname," but because "sir" so aptly reflects the patriarchal bias that Gilman critiques, Gilman's spelling is retained.
5. *Kate Field's Washington* 2 (November 1892): 277.

# 7

# Alimony (1912)

Alimony is the meanest money that is taken—by women. It is bad enough to marry for money; it is bad enough to maintain an immoral marriage for money; but to give up this mercenary commerce and then take money when no longer delivering the goods—! There is only one meanness to be mentioned in the same breath; taking "damages" for "breach of promise."

Some hold it a man's duty to "support" his wife, on the ground that her position as his wife prevents her from earning her living. When she is no longer his wife this does not hold.

Some say that the man should provide for his children; "his" children, note. They are also "hers" surely. But even if he should have the whole burden of their maintenance—that is not "Alimony." Divorcees without children, young women, quite competent to earn their livings, eagerly claim alimony, take it and live on it; never giving a thought to the nature of their position.

But a woman's health is often ruined—she is in no condition to earn her living—is urged.

Very well. If a woman is really injured by her marriage she should sue under the employer's liability act. She should claim damages—not alimony.

# 8

# Competing with Men (1914)

There is no more mischievous phrase in use in connection with the woman's movement than the above. It is a brief and pungent expression, and hits two ways, seeming to involve the women in error both feminine and economic. Such a doubly dangerous catchword should be fully and carefully examined, and dismissed forever from our vocabulary when its absurd falsity is demonstrated. The "men" part of it can be most easily attended to, so we will take that first.

The proposition is that women, in pressing forward into human activities of any sort, and finding men in possession of the entire field, must necessarily come into competition with them, and that this is unwomanly. It is held to put her in a false relation to men, to detract from her womanly charms, to lower her standard and lessen her attractions. Being accepted and believed, it deters many otherwise sensible women from enlarging their field of activities—the all-pervading men having preempted every claim in sight.

Now, the essential error in this position is the universal assumption of mankind that human activities are sex activities—male sex activities, each and all. If they were, it would indeed be unwomanly—and also impossible—for women to attempt competition. A female, as such, cannot compete with a male, as such, their special powers and inclinations being fundamentally different. These common human industries and arts which men are following all over the world have not the faintest relation to sex.

Because women invented sewing, and raised it to a high grade of efficiency, we do not therefore accuse the tailor of "competing with women" because he also practices the art. It is not a male function, but a human function; a process necessary to the development of social life, and open to any member of society.

There is just one occupation on earth which is distinctively masculine, and that is fighting. The business of slaughter belongs by inherent sex-distinction to the male; and there has never been any danger of women's "competing with men" in this field.

The transient condition which gives us today a man-filled business world is not essential; it gives way daily before the steady entrance of women into field after field of previously "masculine" occupation; and presently we may leave out that end of our mischievous phrase, and be confronted only with the statement that "women should not compete." We can withdraw our thought from the supposed error in sex-relation and focus it on the supposed error in economic relation. Here the assumption is this: "Work is done merely to get pay. Work and pay are limited—there is not enough to go around among the people now at work. For a new lot of workers to enter the field would only throw the present workers out of employment, or reduce their wages in proportion to the number of new workers."

This position is honestly and earnestly held by almost all of us; and as the present set of workers happen to be men, and the new set happen to be women, it has a paralyzing effect on the industrial progress of women.

That a given proposition is false, visibly and provably false; that it is ridiculous in its shallow absurdity; that it is without base or backing when fairly studied, and may be instantly overthrown—does not lessen its force in the popular mind. If the majority of the people have been taught a thing a long time and "believe" it—i.e., hold it in the mind without reason—then falsehood and absurdity and little things like that do not matter much. People do not "believe" from a process of reasoning; nor are they likely to disbelieve from such a process. All suffragists know this from experience in their efforts to convince the popular mind by argument.

So it is with no glad smile of triumph that this economic absurdity is laid by—it will bob into place again the moment the weight of the argument is off, and the believers will believe as before.

Here are the modest and unbelieved facts:

The work of the world is necessary to supply the wants and express the powers of the people. So long as there are any people who have powers to express and wants to be supplied, there is work to do. The product of all this work is what we call wealth—the sum of human activity in material form. So long as the earth supplies the requisite materials, the more work there is the more wealth there is. Therefore, the "pay" keeps pace with the work—people work to make things, and the things are distributed in payment for the work, and the more work is done the more wealth there is to distribute in payment.

So every addition to the workers adds to the world's wealth—*they make their own payment and more.*

A hive of a thousand bees would have as much honey as a thousand bees could make. A hive with two thousand bees would have twice as much honey. Imagine the swarm objecting to an accession in numbers on the ground that there was not honey enough to pay them! The bees make the honey—they eat it, of course, but they make more than they eat.

So the working man and woman make wealth; they use some, of course, but they make more than they use.

Therefore, the entrance of the submerged half of the world on the plane of productive industry will pay itself, and add to the world's wealth beside. Now, some thoughtful person, unable to dispute these simple facts, and yet painfully aware that in the business world of today the entrance of women has lowered the wages of men in some cases, will call the above facts "sophistries," will say "That is all true enough in theory, but practically (how fond we are of that word!) it comes out as we say—the women compete with the men and lower their wages!"

The contradiction is admitted, and is thus explained:

In real economic law, the case is as I have stated it. In present economic conditions, the case is as the unthinking observer sees it. Economic laws are permanent. Economic conditions are transient, variable, open to improvement. We arrange them, and we can rearrange them when we will.

If our present economic conditions are unsatisfactory, if they are inimical to the advance of women and the best interests of society, it is for us to study and improve them, holding fast to the permanent underlying laws involved, and altering the transient conditions to suit the facts.

Perhaps the entrance of the non-competitive sex upon the business world may of itself show us the way to better conditions.

Women are pouring forward to take a hand in the world's work because the world needs them and they need it; because such normal social industry develops the woman and enriches the world.

It is a question of human beings, not males and females—of contribution, not competition.

# 9

## These Proud Fathers (1914)

We find valuable newspaper space devoted to long accounts of one Eglinski, Ferdinand Eglinski, a tailor of Ahlbeck, aged fifty-three.[1]

Mr. Eglinski was entertained in Berlin for a week at the expense of the Kaiser, was given a private audience, a fifty-mark note, and the cordial Kaiser is said to have clapped him on the shoulder and cried: "Just keep up the good work, Eglinski!"

He has become a celebrity, this Eglinski, and adds handsomely to his income, we are told, by selling picture postcards of himself.

Now what has Mr. Eglinski done, think you, to deserve all this glory?

He is the father of thirty-five children.

The father.

Not the mother. The two successive wives who bore these thirty-five children are not even named. They were sisters. The first one (Eglinski married at twenty, so she was probably but a girl then) bore twenty-four children.

One woman, of her rich, strong body, brought forth two dozen children. Think of the power, the vigor, the splendid fecundity of this woman who died at about forty-five; who had borne almost a child a year for some twenty-seven years—and then left them when she should have had twenty-five or thirty years more to enjoy life.

Eglinski, appreciating the stock, then married her sister, in the following year; and she, the paper tells us, "has borne him eleven children in the last six years." Triplets once, twins twice.

Note the phrase "has borne him."

Note the innocent, artless, idiotic assumption that Mr. Eglinski is in some mysterious way to be credited with this prodigious fertility! If anyone could doubt it was the woman who was so potent is it not proven by the amazing feat of the second wife—Mr. Eglinski was apparently unable to compass eleven in six years by the first.

Now ask yourself seriously in what way Mr. Eglinski's activity differed from that of any other husband. Had his business separated him from his wife for all but an annual visit, she could have gone on with her mighty task just as well. Of course if he had been absolutely sterile, then he would have been childless, but granting ordinary capacity for fatherhood there's nothing in this great work of womanhood to prove him different from any other man.

Whatever sound man those wonderful sisters had married would have done as well. Perhaps the praise is given for the economic virtues, because of the willingness to support thirty-five children—only nine of whom died. But if he had them to pay for she had them to care for—her work hours were longer than his. That mother of twenty-four must have labored day and night in the service of that limitless family—and built them from her own vitality at the same time.

What the second one has undergone in her whirlwind campaign of eleven in six years it is painful to consider.

But both these mothers are completely ignored by the discerning Kaiser, and in the wide display of this "story" in our press, while the father, whose contribution to their birth was but a momentary pleasure, and whose further labors in their behalf could not have equalled their mother's, is adding to his income by selling picture postcards of himself.

We will not talk about egotism, but how about logic?

## Note

1.    For details, see the article that Gilman most likely read: "Proud Father of 35—Eglinski, German Tailor, Wins the Praise of the Kaiser," *New York Times*, March 28, 1914, p. 4.

# 10

# Without a Husband (1915)

Suppose you haven't a husband; do not want one, perhaps, or for reasons we will not ask, have not been offered one.

Where there are more women than men, as in Massachusetts, there are excellent arithmetical reasons, quite insuperable. A hundred men cannot marry two hundred women, even with all the goodwill in the world; not in Massachusetts, at any rate.

There is such a thing as a woman being too highly educated, or too exactingly pious, or even too beautiful, to be successful in matrimony. The too beautiful one may begin with being vain and hard to please, become more so from too many suitors, and in the end find none to satisfy a too exacting taste.

Anyhow, here you are, thirty-five or forty, and not married—it frequently happens.

Time was when life held out no further hope but to become at best a beloved and valued maiden aunt; next best a dependent poor relation; or, in lower depths, a struggling, impoverished worker, with nameless gulfs below.

That time has gone by.

The "old maid" has given place to the "Bachelor Maid," a pleasant change. In many a line of work today we see unmarried women not only making a living, but making a fortune.

Nevertheless, we find them still less happily adjusted in life than the Bachelor Man. He has his "bachelor apartments," while women are even yet slow to realize that they may have comfortable homes, though husbandless. The man has his friends in warm abundance, while we women are still too near the harem to have that same cordial and varied acquaintance. We are too apt to have an "intimate friend," some single one, deeply loved and all-too-freely confided in, while the man has dozens, and confides to none of them. We are still too much in the Elaineish attitude: "I give thee all in all or not at all!"[1]

But this too is changing. As the lives of women widen and vary, so do their friendships.

The man has his club for relaxation, amusement, comfort. Women have clubs in abundance, but not the same kind. The Women's Clubs[2] of our country are mainly for mental improvement and social service; immensely useful, but not exactly relaxing. Only very lately are they beginning to have real "Living Clubs," with rooms to sleep in, good meals and service, and various games and amusements. There should be such clubs in every town, enough to accommodate each woman who has not what is popularly known as "a home of her own."

Yet she could have even that if she would, and some of them do.

If she will only take time by the forelock, as so often advised, and begin early to work and to save, she may have not only a home, but a child, or children, as much "her own" as the law can guarantee. Not the same thing, of course, as a child one has borne, but wonderfully better than none!

It is rather a reflection on the quality of our mother instinct that so many women without children will deliberately choose the affection of animals, and be contented with their company when there are so many unmothered babies in the world.

Now, why should not a young woman look Fate fairly in the face and plan and work for a Home and an adopted Family of her own, even if she does not marry? It would be a far wholesomer state of mind than of Watchful Waiting, or Asiduous Fishing. And, as a matter of fact, such a woman, so keeping her womanliness alive and warm, might unexpectedly find herself with a husband after all.

A well-reared child is more attractive than a too-fat lap dog.[3]

## Notes

1.     Possibly a reference to two related poems in Alfred Tennyson's *Idylls of the King* (1859), "Merlin and Vivien" and "Lancelot and Elaine." Catherine Adams, surmises,

> In the latter poem, Elaine is a maiden who falls in love with Lancelot. Elaine dies from a broken heart when it is revealed Lancelot cannot love her back.... And, in 'Merlin and Vivien' the character Vivien says the line 'trust me not at all or all in all' three times as a way of seducing Merlin. The first time Vivian says the line she explains that she heard Lancelot sing it once. I suspect that Gilman may have thought the line "I give thee all in all or not at all' appeared

in the 'Lancelot and Elaine" poem instead of the 'Merlin and Vivien' poem....
Or, maybe she meant to say Vivienish instead of Elaineish.

Ms. Adams, M.A.L.S., generously contributed this literary research while working, at the editor's request, on behalf of the University of Nebraska-Lincoln Libraries' Ask a Question Service.

2.  For an encyclopedic account, see Mrs. J.C. Croly, *The History of the Woman's Club Movement in America* (New York: Henry G. Allen, 1898).

3.  Gilman's antipathy toward dogs is manifested in: "On Dogs (1911)," *Sociological Origins* 3 (Autumn 2003): 31-38; and "Dogs, Pigs, and Cities (1916)," *Sociological Origins* 3 (Autumn 2003): 39. By contrast, Gilman's contemporary, sociologist Annie Marion MacLean, strongly favored canines; see "Love My Dog! (1925)," *Sociological Origins* 3 (Autumn 2003): 140-142.

# 11

# The Honor of Bearing His Name (1916)

Someone, writing recently of the high ideals with which a man enters marriage, says that the bride is chosen above all other women for "the honor of bearing his name," and to be the mother of his children.

As to the children, would not the common possessive, "their" be more appropriate and truthful than the single possessive, "His?" "His children" reminds us of the older phrase in which the dutiful child addressed the father as "Author of My Being!"—as if the mother was only the publisher!

But dismissing "his children" with the moderate suggestion that the mother is co-equal in heredity, has the entire task of gestation, parturition, and lactation, and certainly the lion's share of the care, nursing, and education, let us approach with a clear unprejudiced mind this first thing he chose her for—the honor of bearing his name.

Why is it an honor?

Why is his name any more honorable than hers, or, at least, than her father's, which she had the honor of bearing before?

His name was his father's too—a name is not like the Victoria Cross,[1] won by heroism; it is a bequest which we often wish were different.

Suppose we have a father named Jones, with a daughter named Miss Jones, and another father named Brown, with a son Mr. Brown. Of the two fathers, neither has a name more "honorable" than the other. Both are good enough, as names go; not so undesirable as Snooks, nor so impressive as Howard; but one has no advantage over the other.

Then, why, when Miss Jones becomes Mrs. Brown, is she honored by the forced change? Of course, if young Brown had won that name in a foot-race, a boxing-match, or even a guessing contest, he might be a little proud of it, and feel that she would be pleased to have people say:

"There goes Mrs. Brown—*he* was a fine fellow to have that name given him." But even so her pleasure is wholly vicarious; it was by no effort of her own that the noble name was won.

Is the idea that it was by creditable effort on her part that she won him?—the comment being: "It must have taken a pretty clever girl to capture Brown!" At that, he is still the glorious one.

It is, perhaps, still deeper, having no regard to the relative dignity of Brown, Jones, Snooks, or Piddiwiddle; but simply the assumption that any woman is honored by being deprived of her father's name and given a husband's, honored by being chosen at all, by any man.

Here again we are forced to confront the underlying assumption that the man is, *per se*, more "honorable" than the woman, a belief no longer so widespread as formerly. It reminds us of that other sounding phrase, in which a proposal of marriage is called "the highest compliment a man can offer a woman."

Suppose the woman were Jane Addams,[2] a Signora Montessori,[3] some fair crown princess or ruler in her own right, some world-beloved actress or singer. Suppose the man were a sodden tramp, a crook, a criminal, a poor struggling ineffectual peddler of shoestrings. If such a man proposes marriage to such a woman is it a compliment?

How is it? Why is it?

If King Cophetua[4] had been the beggar and The Beggar Maid had been a queen would Tennyson[5] have written the poem about them?

## Notes

1. The Victoria Cross is the highest military honor bestowed on the armed forces in the United Kingdom and Commonwealth countries.
2. Jane Addams (1860-1935) was a noted American sociologist, and a friend of Gilman.
3. Maria Montessori (1870-1952) was a famed Italian educator.
4. King Cophetua is a protagonist in the legend of *The King and the Beggar*.
5. Alfred Tennyson (1809-1892), an English poet, published "The Beggar Maid" in 1842.

# Part III

## Motherhood

# 12

# The New Motherhood (1910)

I have been reading Ellen Key's "Century of the Child,"[1] reviewed in this number, and am moved to add, in connection with that review, a "brief" for the New Motherhood.

Agreeing with almost all of that noble book and with the spirit of the whole of it, I disagree with its persistence in the demand for primitive motherhood—for the entire devotion of each and every mother to her own children—and disagree on the ground that this method is not the best for child service.

Among animals, where one is as good as another, "the mother"—each one of them—can teach her young all that they need to know. Her love, care, and instruction are all-sufficient. In early stages of human life, but slightly differentiated, each mother was still able to give to her children all the advantages then known, and to teach them the few arts and crafts necessary of attainment. Still later, when apprenticeship taught trades, the individual mother was still able to give all the stimulus and instruction needed for early race culture—and did so, cheerfully.

But we have now reached a stage of social development when this grade of nurture is no longer sufficient, and no longer found satisfying either by mother or child. On the one hand, women are differentiating as human beings: they are no longer all one thing—females, mothers, and NOTHING ELSE. They are still females, and will remain so; still mothers, and will remain so: but they are also Persons of widely varying sorts, with interests and capacities which fit them for social service in many lines.

On the other hand, our dawning knowledge of child culture leads us to require a standard of ability in this work based on talent, love, natural inclination, long training, and wide experience. It is no longer possible for the average woman, differentiated or undifferentiated, to fulfill the work of right training for babies and little children, unassisted. Moreover, the New Motherhood is belying today the dogma of the high cultural value of "the home" as a place of education for young children—an old world assumption which Miss Key accepts without question and intensifies.

The standards of the New Motherhood are these:

First: The fullest development of the woman, in all her powers, that she may be the better qualified for her duties of transmission by inheritance.

Second: The fullest education of the woman in all plain truths concerning her great office, and in her absolute duty of right selection—measuring the man who would marry her by his fitness for fatherhood, and holding him to the highest standards in his duty thereto.

Third: Intelligent recognition that child culture is the greatest of arts, that it requires high specialization and life service, and the glad entrance upon this service of those women naturally fitted for it.

Such standards as these recognize the individual woman's place as a human being, her economic independence, her special social service; and hold her a far more valuable mother for such development, able to give her children a richer gift by inheritance than the mothers of the past—all too much in femininity and too little in humanity.

A mother who is something more—who is also a social servant—is a nobler being for a child to love and follow than a mother who is nothing more—except a home servant. She is wiser, stronger, happier, jollier, a better comrade, a more satisfying and contented wife; the whole atmosphere around the child at home is improved by a fully human mother.

On the second demand, that of a full conscious knowledge of the primal conditions of her business, the New Motherhood can cleanse the world of most of its diseases, and incidentally of many of its sins. A girl old enough to marry is old enough to understand thoroughly what lies before her and why.

Especially why. The real cause and purpose of the marriage relation, parentage, she has but the vaguest ideas about—an ignorance not only absurd but really criminal in the light of its consequences. Women should recognize not only the personal joy of motherhood, which they share with so many female creatures, but the social duty of motherhood and its unmeasured powers. By right motherhood they can build the world: by wrong motherhood they keep the world as it is—weak, diseased, wicked.

The average quality of the human stock today is no personal credit to the Old Motherhood, and will be held a social disgrace by the New. But beyond a right motherhood and a right fatherhood comes the whole field of social parentage, one phase of which we call education. The effect of the environment on the child from birth is what demands the attention of the New Motherhood here: How can we provide right conditions for our children from babyhood? That is the education problem. And here arises the insistent question: "Is a small, isolated building, consecrated as a restaurant and dormitory for one family, the best cultural environment for the babyhood of the race?"

To this question the New Motherhood, slowly and timidly, is beginning to answer, "No." It is becoming more and more visible, in this deeper, higher demand for race improvement, that we might provide better educational conditions for the young of the human species. For the all-engrossing importance of the first years of childhood, it is time that we prepared a place. This is as real a need as the need of a college or school. We need A PLACE FOR BABIES—and our homes arranged in relation to such places.

A specially prepared environment, a special service of those best fitted for the task, the accumulated knowledge which we can never have until such places and such service are given—these are demanded by the New Motherhood.

For each child, the healthy body and mind; the warm, deep love and protecting care of its own personal mother: and for all children, the best provision possible from the united love and wisdom of our social parentage. This is not to love our children less, but more. It is not to rob them of the life-long devotion of one well-meaning average woman, but to give them the immortal, continued devotion of age after age of growing love and wisdom from the best among us who will give successive lives to the service of children because they love them better even than their mothers!

## Note

1.   Ellen Karolina Sofia Key (1849-1926), Swedish feminist writer. Her major books include *Love and Marriage* (1911), *The Century of the Child* (1909), and *The Woman Movement* (1912). She is best known for *The Century of the Child*, which Gilman reviewed in *The Forerunner* 1 (December 1910): 25-26. See also Selection 13, below, in which Gilman engaged Key in a direct critique.

# 13

# Education for Motherhood (1913)

In the July and August *Atlantic* the great Swedish feminist, Ellen Key, has an essay in two detachments, on "Education for Motherhood."[1]

In the first of these she once more exhibits either persistent refusal, or incapacity, to fairly state the views of those who hold that the right rearing of babies and small children requires the assistance of specially trained experts, and of an environment beyond that of the average home.

Her error is the same as that of the ordinary unthinking person: she assumes that the additional special care and additional special environment suggested, are not *additional*, but *alternative*—that if that baby has a "baby-garden" to go to, and a "baby-gardener" to care for him, he therefore becomes practically an exile and an orphan.

In her résumé of the abhorred theory, in the opening of this article, she makes sweeping summary of the proposed changes, as "the rearing and educating of children outside the home," the parents to "be supplanted by trained and 'born' educators," and adds that "the children would stand in a visiting relation to the individual home." Further she says that believers in this proposed system hold that "The child's need of the mother and the mother's need of the child is a prejudice which must vanish with all other superstitions from lower stages of culture, if the mothers are to be co-equal with men, community members, capable of work, and if the children are to be well-reared for the social vocations which must soon determine the trend of all lives."

"This program," she continues,

rests on three unproven and undemonstrable assumptions: first, that woman's mental and spiritual work in the home, the creating of a home atmosphere, the management of the housekeeping, and the upbringing of children, is of no "productive value"; secondly, that parents are incapable of acquiring proficiency as educators unless they are "born" educators; thirdly, that nature amply provides such "born" educators, so that the many thousands of institutions—with a professional mother for about every twenty children—could be supplied with them in sufficient quantity and of excellent quality.

So sure is Miss Key that she has rightly defined the theory she opposes that she says: "Of the real outcome of this plan a prominent American woman gave me a touching illustration. As sole support of her son she had been compelled to send him to a boarding school where many little motherless boys were brought up. When she went to visit her boy, the other boys fought with him for a place on her lap, so hungry were they for a moment's sensation of motherly affection."

Before trying to make clear a disagreement it is well to establish all common ground as far as possible, and since Miss Key gives my name as the person responsible for the theory, I will frankly call it mine for the purposes of this argument, though I am not its inventor by thousands of years.

I quite agree with Miss Key as to the ill effects of a mother working outside the home *while no better provision is made for her children than she could make by remaining in it*. This I have said and written for long years.

Also, we agree in the need of a transformed society. She says in this article: "But without such radical social transformation a renaissance of the family life is not even conceivable." This transformed society which, to her mind, will so pay or pension mothers that they may stay at home, will, to my mind, so reduce the hours of labor that the mother need not be away from home more than four hours a day, and further, with the industrial activity of women always counted upon, will so arrange the conditions of labor that the home and the work will not be far apart.

Again, I quite agree with Miss Key in her definition of the "wise educator," never one who is "educating" from morning to night. "She is one who, unconsciously to the children, brings to them the chief sustenance and creates the supreme conditions for their growth. Primarily she is the one who, through the serenity and wisdom of her own nature, is dew and sunshine to growing souls. She is one who understands how to demand in just measure, and to give at the right moment. She is one whose desire is law, whose smile is reward, whose disapproval is punishment, whose caress is benediction." But I flatly disagree with the idea that every mother, meaning, generally, every woman, is—or ever can be—such a benign prodigy.

I agree again, most sincerely, with all the deep universal need of "the child for the mother and the mother for the child." I deny, however, that this need exists in one unbroken, unrelaxing strain, every hour of the day and night. The child does need the mother, the mother does need the child; but both are better off for certain breaks in their companionship. When the baby is asleep, when the children are at school, when they are all in bed at night, then even the motherliest mother can breathe a little more freely, and refresh her mind by other occupations.

Both Miss Key and myself agree in demanding a higher standard of education for young children.

The great disagreement between us is in her assumption that this high standard may be attained by every woman—in one year's study.

In the second instalment of her article she lays down her definite proposition of education for motherhood. Women are to give a year to social service as men do in their military training. Motherhood is here classified as social service. (Here let me stop to smile at this instance of our general attempt to keep women in the same old restrictions. With new education and new growth they are rising and pushing, the world over, saying: "We are tired of everlasting confinement to the kitchen, nursery and parlor, to this one identical round of duties for every woman on earth. We differ, as men differ. We want some variety in action. We want to get out of this eternal domestic service and take part in social service." And those who so long to stop this natural growth, cry to them: "Go back—go back where you were before! That is social service!")

To return to Miss Key's position: Boys and girls are to go to school until fifteen. Then both boys and girls are to study their professions for five years. Then the year of social service, which for the boys is military, and for the girls, training for motherhood.

And what is this training? For five years they have been learning some profession—it is hard to see what for, unless they expect to take it up after the age of fifty perhaps. Then in one year they are to study this:

1. "A theoretic course in natural economics, hygienic and fundamental aesthetic principles for the planning of a home and the running of a household. (Sewing and cooking she assumes to have been learned in school).

2. "A theoretic course in hygiene, psychology, and education for normal children, with some directions for the recognition of abnormalities.

3. "A theoretic course in the physical and psychical duties of a mother before the birth of a child, and the fundamental principles of eugenics."[2]

"To these theoretic courses must be added practical training in the care of children; which knowledge of the child's proper nourishment, clothing and sleep; its physical exercise, play, and other occupations, and its care in case of accident."

There! This is what our prospective mothers are to learn, our young women, all of them, in the space of one year! Five have been allowed them to learn that unaccountable profession which is not to be practiced for some thirty years—if ever; one is allowed to cover this slight field.

And how, where, of whom, are they to learn these manifold arts and sciences?

Here we come to something so funny that I chuckle as I read it, as I copy it accurately from Miss Key's words:

"Children's asylums, day-nurseries, and hospitals, and mother-homes (where mothers with children would find refuge for longer or shorter periods) would give opportunity for such training, led by the teachers."

Has anyone so little sense of logic and sense of humor as not to laugh at this?

In the first half of her article, with a rich profusion of fine language and exalted sentiment, she strives to show the great superiority of "the home" to the carefully planned "baby-garden," attended by the little ones from near-by homes, presided over by those "born educators" she so persistently scoffs at; and similarly to show the superiority of "the mother" to this ridiculed "born educator" (who would be a mother herself most often, but having an extra degree of love for children as children, besides her instinctive love for her own as her own). In the second article, having recognized the glaring fact that motherhood *per se* does not prove competence, that the right care of children does require some definite knowledge as well as all those sacred emotions, she plans this elaborate course of study, crowded into one year's space, crammed into the head of every girl regardless of aptitude; and then, for this instruction, takes her flock to the very worst forms of child grouping—those despised "institutions" in which we now make shift to give some social care to the poorest, weakest, lowest kind of children!

My opponent, without knowing it, thus concedes my whole case.

"Motherhood" in itself does not confer knowledge or capacity; if it did there would be no need of study or training.

For the study and training necessary we are told to go not to "the home," not to "the mother," but to the very institutions whose deadly effects have been so bitterly enlarged upon in the previous pages.

On reading the first half of this article, I took down *Women and Economics*[3] and looked carefully to see if by any chance there was in it anywhere a justification for this perverse misrepresentation. No. Wherever I have referred to the hope of better methods in baby culture I have always taken pains to state that the mother would not be "separated from the child" any more than now when our children, slightly older, go to kindergarten and school.

Miss Key evidently has no objection to that degree of separation, as she clearly allows for school going to the age of fifteen.

By what logical right then does she consider a few hours spent outside the home, by a baby, as more devastating in its influence than the same hours spent, later, in school? By what logical right does she heap scorn on the idea that about one woman in twenty is a "born educator," and then claim that twenty women out of twenty are competent for that work—at least after a year's training; and then, for that training, send them to the despised specialists, not indeed "born" but merely hired, ordinary functionaries of hospitals and asylums?

Once more, wearily but patiently, I will state my position:

Motherhood is a physical and psychical relation, common to all females, highest in ours.

Education is a function having its pre-human beginnings in motherhood, but now a social process, second to none in high importance.

Any normal woman can be a mother, as any normal man can be a father; but every woman cannot be an educator any more than every man can be a musician.

Every normal woman should be a mother, bearing children, nursing them herself, loving them all she is able, teaching them all she is able, and providing for them such care as she cannot herself furnish. (In this last great department of child care the father should assist. At present [s]he does it all—that is, [s]he provides such schooling and special instructions as the child gets).

Every child should grow up in its own home, with its own family, in a separate house, with its own garden when possible.

But—here is the Great Divergence: Every child, as a member of society, is entitled to social care and provision quite outside of and beyond the family care and provision. As we, collectively, establish great universities, colleges and schools, for our children, so we should prepare child gardens, numerous and convenient, where all our little ones could have their special guardians, special playgrounds, special care, and special educational environment—beyond that of the home.

What scarlet headline capitals must I use to show that going to such a place for part of the day does *NOT* deprive a child of home and mother? What detailed and repeated description can reach the public mind, and convince it that a neighboring baby-garden with a small group of happy, well-loved little ones is *NOT* an orphan asylum nor an infant hospital?

The story of the little boys and the visiting mother is an excellent illustration, not at all of the baby-garden theory but of Miss Key's misunderstanding. Here a mother is compelled to send her little son to a boarding school. No such arrangement is involved in my position, which assumes only that the baby shall be in the baby-garden while the mother is doing her four hours' work, and shall be at home when she is.

No one calls a child in the kindergarten a homeless exile, robbed of his mother's love; why consider the baby as such? Is it incapacity to understand which perpetuates this misrepresentation, or conscious unfairness?

Miss Key may sneer at the "born educator," but it remains true that the special genius for child care is not common to all women, and is found in some. It is not as rare as the genius of the great artist or musician, but quite frequent enough to provide for little ones a grade of training far higher than the present, and to provide for the women who possess it a life of fruitful joy.

Given, first, the kind of woman who really enjoys the care and guidance of little children enough to give her life to it; given, second, not one year's crammed confusion of "education for motherhood," but many years of wide study, and of careful preliminary practice; given, third, a place which is meant to provide peace, beauty and unconscious education for the opening soul; given, fourth, a long succession of grouped little ones to observe and learn from—and we shall at last begin to lay the foundations of the real science of baby culture.

Then indeed there will be some "education for motherhood." All mothers, in daily contact with higher methods, may begin to improve their own. The standards of child culture will rise from year to year by the purely natural process of observation and experience.

No unpracticed individual theorist can teach mothers sufficiently. No one mother, enriched only by her own experience with her own children, can teach other mothers sufficiently.

The accumulated learning of doctors, nurses, and pedagogues can give us information on their specific lines, but how to rear a baby not only in physical health, but in soul-health, with the maximum of development and the minimum of nerve-waste, can never be taught until it is learned, and can never be learned until serious, life-long study and practice is given to it.

There are two inexorable limitations to the work of the individual mother, which I once more repeat.

One is this: Even if every mother had the talent—which they have not; even if every mother took the exhaustive course of training requisite—which they will not; still, so long as each mother takes all the care of her own children, no one can ever have the requisite *experience*.

You do not want doctor or dentist or dressmaker to *begin on you*. You expect of them previous practice—under the eyes of experts, the more the better.

In all other human work we have the benefit of the accumulated progressive experience of the ages. Only the culture of babies—most important of all work—is left to that eternal amateur—the mother.

The other paradox is this: Suppose we have an individual mother possessed of all three requisites, talent, training, *and* experience; that is, a woman who had fitted for the position of baby-gardener and held it long, but who finally decides to withdraw from that position and consecrate her services to her own baby at home.

Such ceaseless focussing of professional ability upon one child, or a few, is too intense an atmosphere for little ones to unfold in. The mother-and-child relation should be kept wholesomely unstrained, and the teacher-and-child relation also. To share with many other little ones the wise supervision of the teacher for part of the day, and to return fresh and eager to the love of an as fresh and eager mother, is far more healthful.

Any mother who is capable of giving all that a child needs, and keeps such unusual power exclusively for her own, is a social traitor.

## Notes

1. Key's two-part article on "Education for Motherhood" appeared in the *Atlantic Monthly*, Vol 112 (July 1913: 48-56) and (August 1913: 191-197). The article, originally written in Swedish, was especially translated into English for the *Atlantic Monthly*.
2. Eugenics, a perspective recognizing that controlled breeding practices can increase the occurrence of desired heritable characteristics in a population. Gilman advised women to consider the genetic makeup of potential mates, especially with a view to avoiding the perpetuation of genetically transmitted diseases.
3. Charlotte Perkins Stetson [Gilman], *Women and Economics: A Study of the Economic Relation between Men and Women as a Factor in Social Evolution* (Boston: Small, Maynard & Company, 1898).

# 14

## "Wanted— Young Girl to Mind Baby and Do Light Housework" (1914)

Well—what is there unusual about that? Nothing. It is perfectly usual, common, universal.

The young girl is very young, in this case, just an extra. She is very ignorant, and of poor extraction—else she wouldn't do it.

But that is not material. She may be 13 or 14—with all a child's limitations; she may have had but little broken schooling and no other education; she may have had—probably has had—the lowest of home influences and street or shop influence as well. She may not be worth more than the $2 a week she will get—if she gets that. But she is quite competent, in the mind of the divinely endowed mother of the family, "to do light housework" and to "mind the baby."

The light housework—dusting, dishwashing, setting the table, preparing the vegetables, making bed. Nothing of importance here—only the health and comfort of the family, and somewhat of its prosperity.

Minding the baby—taking it out in the little carriage, watching it while it toddles about, staying in the house while the mother is out, or otherwise engaged—that's all. She is not the final arbiter of the baby's health and education; that supreme power is with the divinely endowed aforesaid; but she does have charge of the baby for a good many hours, when the mother is absent from her home.

And how many of those all-important first impressions, how many answers to first questions, how many strange and vivid tales, how many exhibitions of irresponsible authority does this young girl contribute to the unfolding brain she has charge of? What a comment it is on our motherhood—what a glaring, ghastly proof of our incompetence that we should think the care of a child of such small moment, a thing to be done by a "young girl" in the interval of "light housework!"

# 15

# Birth Control (1915)

The time will come when every nation must face the question, "How many people can live comfortably, healthfully, happily, upon this land?" That is the ultimate reason why we must learn that "the pressure of population" is not an unavoidable fate, but a result of our own irresponsible indulgence.

This time is still a long way off. At present the main reasons advanced in advocacy of the conscious limitation of offspring are these: the economic pressure which often makes it difficult, if not impossible, to rear large families without degradation of the stock from injurious conditions; the injury to women of a continuous repetition of maternity, especially when combined with hard work and lack of comfort; and back of these, less freely stated, a desire for "safe" and free indulgence of the sex instinct without this natural consequence.

Of the first reason it may be said that the economic pressure is our own making and may be removed when we choose. That a race of our intelligence should sink into conditions so miserable that it is difficult to raise healthy children; and then, instead of changing those miserable conditions, should weakly renounce parentage, is not creditable to that intelligence. While we have not come within centuries of "the limit of subsistence"; while there is land enough and water enough to feed a vast population as yet unapproached; it is contemptible for us to accept mere local and temporary injustice as if it were a natural condition. That the more ignorant masses should do this would not be strange; but they are not the main culprits. So far they have faced the evils around them with nature's process—the less chance of a living, the more young ones.

Wiser people, more far-seeing, with a higher standard of living to keep up, have accepted their restrictions as final, and sought to limit their own numbers as to maintain that standard for the few.

If we would apply our reasoning power and united force to secure a fair standard of living for all of us, we could go on enjoying our families for many centuries. In the meantime, accepting our present limitations, we do have to face the very practical and personal problem—how many children ought a woman to have whose husband's wages average $600 a year. That is the average for millions, even in our country.

Face this fairly: $2.00 a day for all but the fifty-two Sundays, say three holidays, and a most modest allowance of ten days' unemployment—less than $12.00 a week the year around, with rent and food prices what they are now. How many children *ought* a woman to have under these circumstances?

Then, either for this woman, overworked and underfed; or for the professor's wife, also overworked in the demands of her environment; and, though having enough to eat, also underfed in the rest and relaxation she needs; we must face the limitations of physical strength.

Here again, in a large sense, our position is pusillanimous. Maternity is a natural process. It should benefit and not injure the mother. That women have allowed themselves to sink into a condition where they are unfit to perform the very functions for which their bodies are specially constructed, is no credit to their intelligence. Instead of accepting the limitations and saying: "We are not strong enough to bear children," the wise and noble thing to do is to say: "Our condition of health is shameful. We must become strong and clean again that we may function naturally as mothers."

In spite of this, the practical and personal problem confronts the individual mother: "I have had three children in three years. I am a wreck already. If I have another I may die or become a hopeless invalid. Is it not my duty for the sake of those I have, to refuse to have more?"

The third reason, by no means so outspoken, but far more universal than the others, is at once the strongest force urging us toward birth control, and the strongest ground of opposition to it.

The prejudice against the prevention of conception and the publication of knowledge as to the proper methods, is based partly on religious conviction, and partly on an objection to the third reason above given. The religious objection is neither more nor less difficult to meet than others of the same class. A wider enlightenment steadily tends to disabuse our minds of unthinking credulity as to ancient traditions. We are beginning at last to have a higher opinion of God than we used to entertain. The modern mind will not credit an Infinite Wisdom, an Infinite Love, with motives and commands unworthy the love and wisdom of a mere earthly father. Still, for those who hold this objection, and upon whom it is enforced by their Church, it is a very serious one.

The other is still more serious; so much so that no one can rightly judge the question without squarely facing this, its biological base—what is sex union for. No one can deny its original purpose, its sole purpose through all the millions of years of pre-human life on earth. But when human life is under consideration there are two opinions.

The first holds that the human species is sui generis[1] in this regard; that we differ from all other animals in this process; that it has, for us, both a biological use quite aside from reproduction, and a psychological use entirely beyond that.

The second is to the effect that for our race, as for others, this is a biological process for the perpetuation of the species, and that its continuous indulgence with no regard to reproduction or in direct exclusion of reproduction indicates an abnormal development peculiar to our species.

The first opinion is held by practically everyone; the second by a mere handful. To those who have watched the growth of ideas in the human mind this disproportion proves nothing whatever. Of course a few people are as likely to be wrong as a great many people. Of course a small minority of people have held views as absurd as those of large majorities. Nevertheless it remains true that every advance in all human history has been begun by the ideas of a few, even of one perhaps, and opposed with cheerful unanimity by all the rest of the world.

An idea must be discussed on its merits, not measured by the numbers of people who "believe" this, or "think" that, or "feel" so and so. Especially as to feeling. The emotional responses of the mass of people are invariably reactionary. "Feelings," which belong to a more advanced state, are always hard to find. Even in one's own mind, the intellectual perception comes first, the settled conviction later, and the appropriate emotional response later still.

One may be fairly forced by sheer reason and logic to admit the justice and expedience of equal suffrage for men and women; one may accept this as a strong belief and act accordingly. Yet the swift warm sense of approval for what is still called a "womanly woman," the cold aversion to what we have for long assumed to be "unwomanly," remain.

Because of these simple and common phenomena, we must not be swayed too much in our judgment on this question as to the true use and purpose and the legitimate limits of the sex function, by the overwhelming mass of sentiment on the side of continuous indulgence.

For clear discussion it will be well to state definitely the thesis here advanced, which is:

That with the human species as with others the normal purpose of sex-union is reproduction;

That its continuous repetition, wholly disassociated with this use, results in a disproportionate development of the preliminary sex emotions and functional capacities, to the detriment of the parental emotions and capacities, and to the grave injury of the higher processes of human development;

That our present standard of "normal indulgence" is abnormal; this by no means in the sense of any individual abnormity, but in the sense of a whole race thus developed by thousands of generations of over-indulgence;

That, when the human species, gradually modifying its conduct by the adoption of changed ideas, becomes normal in this regard, it will show a very different scale of emotional and functional demand; the element of sex-desire greatly reduced in proportion to the higher development of parental activities worthy of our race; and of a whole range of social emotions and functions now impossible because of the proportionate predominance of this one process and its emotions;

That this change will necessarily be a slow one; and involves, not the pious struggles of a convicted sinner against a sin, but the wise gradual efforts of a conscious race to so change its habits, to so modify itself, as to breed out the tendency to excessive indulgence, and allow the re-assumption of normal habits;

That the resultant status is not of an emasculate or e-feminate race; or of one violently repressing its desires; but rather that of a race whose entire standard has changed; in physical inclination, in emotion, and in idea; so that the impulse to that form of sex-expression comes only in a yearly season, as with other species of the same gestative period.

The opposing thesis is so universally held as hardly to need statement, but may be fairly put in this way:

That it is "natural" for the human species to continually indulge sex-emotion and its physical expression, with no regard whatever to reproduction.

That this indulgence has "a higher function" in no way associated with so crude a purpose as bringing forth children, but is (a) an expression of pure and lofty affection; (b) a concomitant of all noble creative work; (c) a physical necessity to maintain the health of men—some say also of women.

This position is reinforced not only by the originally strong sex instinct in all animals, and by the excessive force of that instinct in the human race; but by the world's accumulated psychology on the subject—its pictures, statues, stories, poems, music, drama, even its religions, all of which have been elaborated by the sex which has the most to gain and the least to lose by upholding such a standard.

Without expecting to make much impression upon such a measureless mass of instinct, sentiment, habit, and tradition, we may offer this much consideration of the above position.

First, as to the use of the word "natural." The forces of nature tend to preserve life—under any conditions. Up to the last limits of possibility, the form, size, and structure, habits, and feelings of a living species, will change and change and change again in order that it may live. Anything will be sacrificed—so that the one main necessity is maintained—that the creature be not extinct. "Nature," in the sense of creatures below mankind, often failed in this effort, and many species did become extinct. Our human conditions, which are natural too but not in this special sense, are so favorable that human life is maintained where less able creatures would die.

It is quite possible for a part of society to so conduct itself as would inevitably cause its own destruction if it were not meanwhile fed and clothed and sheltered by another part. It is possible for quite a small fraction of society to promote ideas, theories, and habits which would corrupt and degrade the whole if they were not offset by other tendencies. In the specific matter in question, the one absolute condition of life was merely this: that enough women reached the bearing age and produced enough children to maintain the race in existence.

The condition of said race might be as low as that of the fellaheen[2] of Egypt, of the Australian savage, of the Bushman of Africa. No matter—if they still live, "Nature" seems to be satisfied.

Moreover, we may say that so universal a habit as the use of alcohol is "natural," meaning that it is easily adopted by all races and classes of men. To call a thing "natural" in that sense does not show it to be advantageous.

As to the "higher function," we should be clear in our minds about the relation between the "height" of the function and its frequence. It may be advanced, similarly, that eating with us, has a "higher function," being used as a form of hospitality, a medium of entertainment, of aesthetic as well as gustatory pleasure. All that may be true of the preparation, service, and consumption of food which is perfectly suited to the needs of the body, and for which one has a genuine appetite. One would hardly seek to justify a ceaseless gluttony, or even an erratic consumption of unnecessary food, on those grounds.

It remains further to be discussed in detail whether noble and lofty affection may not be otherwise expressed; whether it is true that the highest creative work, or the most, or even any great part, is associated with our present degree of indulgence on this line; and whether that claim of "physical necessity" really holds good for either sex.

It may be shown that a person, today, is in better health if free to gratify his present degree of desire; but that is not the real point at issue, which is—is it normal for the human race to have this degree of desire?

Against the visible sum of our noble achievements, which may be urged as justification of our peculiarities, may be set the as visible sum of our shameful diseases, sufferings, poverty, crime degeneracy. As a race we do not show such an exceptionally high average of health and happiness in the sex relation as to indicate a "higher" method. Rather, on the contrary, the morbid phenomena with which this area of life is associated, plainly show some wrong condition.

Upon which general bias, returning to the subject of birth control, it is advanced: That the normal sex relation is a periodic one, related to the reproductive process;

That the resultant "natural" product of a child a year is being gradually reduced by the action of that biological law—"reproduction is in inverse proportion to individualization";

That when we are all reared in suitable conditions for the highest individual development, we shall only crave this indulgence for a brief annual period, and that, with no efforts at "prevention," our average birth rate will be but two or three to a family;

That, in the meantime, under specially hard conditions, it is right for a woman to refuse to bear more than that, or possibly to bear any;

That for reputable physicians or other competent persons to teach proper methods of such restrictions, is quite right.

As for needing a "safe," free, and unlimited indulgence in the exercises of this function, I hold that to be an abnormal condition.

## Notes

1.  *Sui generis*, a Latin term meaning "of its own kind" or "belonging to a class of things peculiar to itself."
2.  Fellaheen, peasants or agricultural workers in an Arabic-speaking country, such as Egypt.

# Part IV

## Children and Parents

# 16

## Prize Children (1910)

A prosperous farmer, driving a valuable horse, will exhibit with pride the "points" of his swift roadster—the fine action, the speed and endurance. He himself sits stoop-shouldered and muscle-bound; strong, it may be, but slow and awkward; with bad teeth and poor digestion; by no means a model human being either in "points" or "action."

He never thinks of these things.

A virtuous housewife, running a comfortable house, has a justifiable pride in the cleanliness, comfort, and convenience of the place, in its beautiful appointments and conveniences, and in her own fine clothes! She herself is stout, short-legged, incapable of any swift agility of action; a brief run leaves her panting; she would be grotesque as a statue; and her internal housekeeping is by no means as efficient as a doctor would approve.

She never thinks of these things.

The same farmer will show you his stock—sheep, swine, fowls, cattle; point out their superiority and talk learnedly of the best methods of improvement. The same housewife will show you her fine needlework, her fine cooking, and discuss patterns and recipes with gusto. Both the farmer and his wife took prizes at the county fair—he for pigs and poultry, she for pies.

Now look at their children.

She gathers little Johnny into her motherly arms. "Johnny was always delicate!" she says tenderly. "He's a little backward because he's delicate. Mother's boy!" And she kisses his smooth head as he nestles up to her. "Adelaide had better go and lie down. Adelaide's not strong. They work her too hard in school."

Jim looks sturdy enough, and makes noise enough, but the expert perceives that Jim has adenoids, breathes through his mouth, is really undersized.

Here is the oldest boy, a tall, heavy fellow; but what a complexion! "Quite natural for boys of that age; yes, he's real sensitive about it."

---

Well? They are "good children." When properly dressed, they compare favorably with other people's children.

None of them would take any prizes in an exhibition of Human Stock. There are no such prizes. As to the exhibition—that is continuous. We are so used to the exhibition, and to its pitiful average, that we have no ideals left.

Neither the farmer nor his wife ever thought of a Human Standard; whether they came up to it, or if their children did, or of how they might improve the breed.

We take humanity as we find it. We admire "beauty," or what we call beauty; but we don't care enough for it to try to increase it. We are concerned about our health after we lose it, but give small thought to lifting the average. Young men vie with one another in athletic sports, and have certain ideals, perhaps, of "military bearing," and the kind of chest and chin a man should have; but all their ideals put together do not make us as beautiful and strong as we have a right to be.

Then arise those who come to us talking largely of eugenics; wanting us to breed super-men and super-women; talking largely of eugenics; wanting us to [improve] the race by right selection. There is a lot of sense in this; we could do wonders that way; of course, if we would. Certain obstacles arise, however. Men and women seem to love each other on other grounds than physical superiority. Those physically superior do not always have the most superior children. Then, again, the physically superior children do not always hold out through life, somehow.

This method of breeding and selection is nature's way. It works well—give it a chance; but it has to be accompanied by a ruthless slaughter of the unfit, and takes thousands upon thousands of years. We have a method worth two of that.

We can improve the species after it is born.

That's the great human power, the conscious ability to improve ourselves and our children. We have the power. We have the knowledge, too—some of us have it, and all of us can get it.

The trouble is, speaking generally, that we haven't the standards.

Here is where our mothers need new ideals, and new information. A person who is going to raise cattle ought to know something about cattle; know what to expect of cattle, and how to produce it. Suppose we had a course in Humaniculture to study. We have Agricultural colleges; we study Horticulture, and Floriculture, and Apiculture and Arboriculture. Why not have a Humanicultural College, and learn something about how to raise people?

Such a course of study would begin with the theory, illustrating by picture and model; and later should have practical illustration from the living model, in nursery and school. The graduate from such a course would have quite a different idea of human standards.

She would know the true proportions of the human body, and not call a No. 2 foot "beautiful" on a No. 10 body. She would know what the real shape of the human body is, and that to alter it arbitrarily is a habit of the lowest savagery. The shape of the body is the result of its natural activities, and cannot be altered without injury to them. She would learn that to interfere with the human shape, molding it to lines that have nothing to do with the living structure and its complex functions, is as offensive and ridiculous as it would be to alter the shape of a horse.

Should we not laugh to see a horse in corsets? The time is coming when we shall so laugh to see a woman.

She would learn to measure beauty, human beauty, by full health and vigor first of all, right proportion, full possession of all natural power, and that the human animal is by nature swift, agile, active to a high degree, and should remain so throughout life. So trained, she would regard being "put on a car" by the elbow as an insult, not a compliment.

Then at last we should begin to have some notion of what to expect in children, and how to get it. The girl would look forward not merely to some vague little ones to love and care for, but to having finer children than anyone else—if she could! And she would naturally have a new standard of fatherhood, and sternly refuse to accept disease and the vice which makes disease.

Then, when the children came, she would know the size and weight that was normal, the way to feed and clothe the little body so as to promote the best growth; the kind of exercise and training essential to develop that legitimate human beauty and power which ought to belong to all of us.

We have our vulgar "Baby Shows," where fat-cheeked, over-fed younglings are proudly exhibited. A time is coming when, without public exhibitions, without prize-money or clamorous vote, we shall raise a new standard in child culture—and live up to it.

# 17

# Is There a Double Standard in Filial Duty?
# (1912)

Filial duty is not so deeply based as a good many others.[1] It has not the primitive necessity of parental duty, on which rests the very life of any race, nor the high glory of social duty, upon which follows all our further progress. It is a sort of handmade duty, developed to meet occasion. When the life of the tribe demanded physical fitness of every individual, the old savage met neglect and death as philosophically as an old bear or wolf. He knew that if he was unable to keep himself alive he must die, that was all. But when our growing humanness brought out new mental powers, and the accumulated wisdom of the old was of service to the young; then grew the adage: "Old men for counsel, young men for war," and it became advisable to keep the old alive.

From this modest and practical beginning sprang all our customs of respect for the aged, of filial duty, and of ancestor worship. With the prolongation of infancy and adolescence, the need of parentage has been prolonged; with private property and the right to bequeath it, parentage acquired new power; with the heavy sanction of time-honored religion we deified the word "father," and, in practice, "mother" was nearly as much revered.

All this is deeply embedded in our minds. Meanwhile the customs of our lives have changed; our economic conditions have changed; our social relationship and our consciousness of that relationship is changing fast. The state does more and more for the young citizen; the parent proportionately less. Upon this should follow an increase in the sense of civic honor, gratitude, and duty; with a commensurate gradual lessening of filial duty. On the other hand, as the service of individuals is seen to be not merely to keep families alive, but to maintain the state, there rises a new recognition of the state's duty to the aged; and old-age pensions are appearing, in slow recognition of that claim.

In this new status the parent should no longer regard service of children as a forced loan, holding it over their heads as an obligation, and demanding its full return; exacting also a respect and affection based only on the relationship—not on character.

The parental service of children is a natural duty, only partially superseded by the state service of children; parental duty can never cease; but it should not be considered as a mortgage on a child's life.

The reverse obligation, in which the young are heavily burdened by the support and care of the old, may be nobly and cheerfully borne by the child, but is felt as a painful dependence by any self-respecting parent. To have to give up one's own housekeeping, or one's own business, and go and live on one's children as a dependent grandfather, or grandmother, is a situation difficult to bear gracefully. It is not always borne gracefully. In those Oriental races where this is the highest of duties, it is made as pleasant as possible for the aged, but results in cruel injustice to the young—a sort of shameful slavery. With us it is easier for the young, but by no means so pleasant for the old. No one likes to be a burden, and in especial no one likes to be a burden upon those one loves best and would most wish to help.

Like every other problem in life this presses most hardly on the poor. If there is great wealth the parents may keep their own homes, or travel with "companions," or go to comfortable and expensive sanitariums. If there is moderate wealth there is at least room in the house for grandma or grandpa, and no one is incommoded. But for the poor, where crowding little ones claim every mouthful of food, every inch of space, the mere providing of food and shelter for the old folks is an injury to the young—and both feel it.

Against this difficulty, solving and settling it as it does so many others, rises the new recognition of social status. Because this industrial soldier has served the country for so long, he, or she, is now honorably entitled to a pension, and that pension will enlarge with our enlarging social consciousness.

This is the line of development which is gradually removing the burden of filial obligation from the young; and it alone will tend to increase our rate of social progress materially. But while we still have this duty to face; while our parents have labored most for us and as little as possible for the state; perhaps even robbing the state, or cheating in its service, for our benefit; we are bound by necessity, honor, and affection in this old tie of filial duty. We must care for our parents, when they are no longer able to care for themselves.

Now, granting all this, will anyone come forward to explain why a daughter owes more filial duty than a son?

A girl baby is no harder to bring into the world than a boy baby—often easier. A girl child is no harder to bring up than a boy child—almost always easier. The girl has more viability at birth, is less susceptible to disease, less given to naughtiness and mischief, less of a risk through carelessness and rebellion. The girl child, moreover, begins to be useful far earlier than the boy. She helps her mother in her work long before the boy can help his father. She does not, it is true, command so much in wages as her brother, but she brings home a larger proportion of it; and, if the family is poor, she works in the home as well as out.

Even if the family is not poor, she is expected to remain to add to the beauty and grace of home life, while he is quite free to go where business or inclination calls him. If the parental family is broken up; if son or daughter is called upon to undertake the support and care of a surviving parent, the obligation of gratitude and filial duty is, as a matter of fact, precisely equal, except as the boy has been more trouble, and, if a professional man, far more expense.

But we do not consider it equal. If it is in the ancestor-worshipping countries, the bitterness of absolute slavery is upon the daughter and the daughter-in-law, far more than upon the son and son-in-law. In our own land, with all our enlightenment and progress, with quite enough intelligence to see that the obligation is the same in either sex, we still expect quite a different fulfillment. "The dutiful son" must "support" his aged father, his dependent mother; but he supports them by paying bills and hiring servants or nurses. We do not expect of the son that he make himself a nurse or a servant to his aged parent; we do expect it of the daughter. Why? Why this deep-rooted conviction that a woman must do the house-service, the hand-labor?

We are always disguising our conviction, covering it with heaped flowers of sentiment. We call it the "duty of the wife"; "the duty of the mother"; "the duty of the daughter"!; "the duty of the sister"—a woman has to be some relation to a man! Flatly and frankly what we mean is that it is the duty of women, as a sex, to be the domestic servants of the world. This is our double standard of filial duty. He is the son of his parents; she is not only their daughter, but their servant.

# Note

1. For an equally perceptive essay on the tensions between generations, specifically between fathers and daughters, written by one of Gilman's friends and colleagues, see Jane Addams, "Filial Relations," in Addams' *Democracy and Social Ethics* (New York: Macmillan, 1902: 71-101).

# 18

## Illegitimate Children (1913)

It is hard, of course, to realize that a long established custom is not a law of nature. Most of us, growing up to find what we call "life" being run on certain lines, assume that it has to run that way always.

Among the prominent and painful features of this "life" of ours, as we find it, is the care of what are called "illegitimate" children. The shame of the bastard was supposed to be inherent, unavoidable. If anyone called it unjust, we complacently quoted that useful proverb: "The fathers have eaten sour grapes and the children's teeth are set on edge"[1]—and went right on with the grapes.

In our very recent perception that all the previous conditions of society, throughout history, are androcentric, man-made by the men, of the men, and for the men, as we might say, we are now gradually beginning to test one thing after another in the world about us, and see if it really has to be the way it is—or if it is quite unnecessary, and perhaps extremely wrong. In such study we find a veritable sunburst of new light on this whole question of "illegitimate" birth.

In pre-human life no such thing exists, of course; in early human life the customs of low races petrified gradually into morals and varied widely. The virtue of chastity, for instance, was slow in development, and extremely variable. It was almost exclusively confined to women, and among women was first demanded after marriage, later made a requisite before marriage, and is now pretty generally established among civilized races both before and after.

But the requirement in all cases was made by men. They wished their wives to be "true" to them, that they might not father another man's child. The man's assumption that he was the sole transmitter of life made him extremely sensitive about his "name," his "line," and the whole structure of family pride, with its laws of primogeniture and entail, rests on this essentially androcentric—and quite erroneous—idea.

The later masculine demand for premarital chastity on the part of the woman was a requirement based on this same idea, together with the natural jealousy of property rights. When a man asked a woman to be "his," he wanted her all his, and never at any time to have been "another's." Of course, since suitors possessed absolute freedom of selection, and fathers absolute powers of coercion, and since all the modifying influences of religion, education, and the arts, as well as social customs, were in male hands, it was easy to develop this virtue, and it has been done.

Unfortunately, however, men not only wished women to be chaste— for their preferred use in marriage—but they wished them to be un-chaste for their use without marriage, which complicated the problem a good deal. As men were not required to be chaste, this specially developed virtue was contradicted by inheritance—a thing quite unnoticed. A reformed rake was said to make the best husband, and his daughters were expected to be as virtuous as any other man's.

Often married life is not calculated to maintain the spirit of chastity, nevertheless the wife of the most self-indulgent husband was expected to remain unassailable by any other man.

Meanwhile a certain proportion of women were maintained in polyandrous and promiscuous relations for the pleasure of men, and though considered undeniably necessary for that pleasure, and as a sort of scapegoat to protect other women by their ceaseless sacrifice, they were made to suffer great misery and shame.

As a class of professionals they were cut off from motherhood for the most part, but another element here enters into the case, and one of singular contemptibility. Not content with the professional class maintained for the express purpose of allowing men to be unchaste, they greatly preferred fresh sacrifices—clean young girls, reared in the "innocence" and virtue meant for marriage. With the full advantage of experience, knowledge and power, as against innocence, ignorance, and weakness, men have continually recruited the rapidly dying class of their professional servants by new victims from the ranks of girlhood.

This process quite naturally resulted in motherhood, and this gives us the problem of "the illegitimate child."

Since the "name," considered such a necessity to honorable life, was wholly man's (women having no names of their own, but merely using the father's till provided with the husband's) and was denied this child born "out of wedlock"; and since the girl's father, offended in his tenderest part—his "honor"—usually scorned and cast off his daughter; since, further, the economic dependence of women, especially of immature girls—the kind always preferred for this experience—rendered it difficult if not impossible for any such young mother to provide proper maintenance for her child, the condition of the blameless baby was hard indeed.

The man's attitude toward the woman in the case is ignoble enough, unreasonable enough, cruel enough, but how does he explain to himself his attitude toward his own child? Especially since he so generally assumed that he was the sole life-giver—she but the nurturer of the seed.

No better instance need be given, could be given, of the unfitness of the male alone to make a just and beneficent society.

The result of his quite unchecked indulgence of masculine tendencies has been to make the world as we know it, with its special field of horrors along this line, and in the case of the illegitimate child, to pour into the world a considerable proportion of children, handicapped from birth, and doomed to a life necessarily robbed of its principal honors and emoluments.

What should be the attitude of the new world, the world of conscious motherhood, toward the illegitimate child? The change is too great to be more than outlined here.

She will require chastity of man, as he has of her, not for her own pride or pleasure, however, but for the good of the race.

She will allow no longer the helpless ignorance of girlhood, so convenient for attack, but rear young women strong in knowledge, full of high pride in their duty of motherhood, determined to uplift humanity by breeding a nobler race. Such will select wisely, with open eyes, as is the duty of the female in all races.

The professional class of prostitutes will disappear with economic independence of women, right education of both sexes, and well-administered new laws, laws such as no wholly male society would ever make or ever administer.

Unprofessional unchastity we must outgrow, more slowly, through education and careful breeding.

As to illegitimate children, the term will disappear from the language.

When women have names of their own, names not obliterated by marriage, that precious male prerogative will no longer be given or withheld at his pleasure; there will be no way of labeling a child at once, as legitimate or otherwise.

When women have money of their own, earned by human work, then a mother can care for her child as a father would, and "illegitimacy" will not mean poverty as well. When women have organized as men have, providing proper conditions for children as men have not—far reaching changes in the whole social world structure—then all children will have a chance to grow to their best.

And a new virtue, a new chastity, a new honor, will arise—the virtue and chastity of a clean, well-controlled parentage; the honor of the woman, the mother, to breed only from the best, to choose her husband wisely and keep pure the race—as the man has tried to keep pure his self-bestowed name.

## Note

1.   See Ezekiel 18:2.

# 19

# My Mother Right or Wrong (1915)

We are beginning to look somewhat askance at the long revered cry "My Country, right or wrong," and we ask ourselves why crime or folly is less to be deprecated when collective than when individual. We are beginning to see that the good of humanity should be our ideal, not that trampling juggernaut of national egotism whose awful work is now in process of exhibition in Europe.

But there are still a large majority who maintain "The Divine Right of Mothers" though they have long outgrown belief in the divine right of kings.

One of these has sent me an expression of the feeling brought out by the Teacher Mother discussion in New York. Her position is strongly against a woman's continuing to teach after she is a mother, and is consummately expressed in her quotation: "No matter how bad a mother may be, her child is better with her than with the best of care from others."

Before a statement like this one sits dumb. Think of it. Read it carefully. Think of how bad a mother has been known to be. Ask the Society for the Prevention of Cruelty to Children.[1] Think of the criminal mothers, the idiot mothers, the millions of ignorant mothers; the shallow, idle, selfish mothers, all too commonly seen.

Then think of "the best of care" from others, not the want of care, the care of overtaxed indifferent hirelings in badly run, crowded public institutions; but the care of earnest, competent, wise, trained women, who love children as children, not merely as their own; and with all this in view we are told that the worst mother is better than this for the child.

A woman who is ignorant does not become wise by the process of childbearing. Those who bear most children often lose most; their mother love does not teach them laws of health, much less laws of infant psychology.

A baby has more chance of life, health, and right development if adopted by a wise and tender woman who knows the work of child caring, than if left in the hands of the worst grade of mothers.

There is held to be some mysterious potency in "Mother love" that shall guard and save the child through all—but does it?

Look at our dirty, weazened, stunted children of the slums; look at the kind of people we raise, the world over. Do not focus your attention upon the few Great Men, to whose Devoted Mothers we always proudly point; but look at the average man and then at the below average—the large class of sick, crippled vicious degenerate weaklings.

They all had mothers, and most of them had "mother's care."

Every backward race, every primitive savage race, every decadent race, has mothers and mother's care.

Only the Forward Races of the world add to their motherhood the higher function of teacherhood, and show the improvement wrought by this larger service.

But when all is said to show that love and wise care are what the child needs, and which is not always properly given by the mother—what has it to do with the Teacher-Mother question.[2]

Simply the old asinine folly which assumes that if a mother works outside the home she thereby ceases to be a mother, ceases to love or care for her children.

Why do not these critics cry out against the women who, being able to afford it, engage trained nurses, governesses, and tutors for their children?

No one points to the wholesale decadence of children thus cared for—because it is not true. No, they bring up this old matriolatrous[3] doctrine merely to oppose the one thing such minds most dread, mothers really free, active, independent; mothers who are self-supporting citizens, and who claim the right to use their own trained judgment in providing right care for their children.

## Notes

1.  The New York Society for the Prevention of Cruelty to Children, the world's first child protective agency, was founded in 1875 by Elbridge T. Gerry.
2.  For the result of court cases concerning removal of female teachers who became mothers, see "Teacher-Mothers Win Final Verdict," *New York Times*, January 12, 1915: 1.
3.  Matriolatrous doctrine, i.e., unreflexive mother worship.

# 20

# Is Childhood Happy? (1916)

There is a general theory to the effect that children are happy just because they are children. We talk of "happy childhood" and sentimentalize about it, often in the hearing of most unhappy youngsters who know better.

It is true that a healthy child enjoys being alive, but so does a healthy grown person. But when a child is unhealthy, as often happens, he or she has none of the comforts of philosophy; neither the vivid memory of a better past, nor the vivid hope of a better future.

It is true that a baby is "pleased by a rattle, tickled by a straw," but so are we pleased and tickled by a variety of more complicated noises and ticklers. But if the baby drops his rattle he can only cry; he can neither pick it up again, nor make another—as we can ours.

Children's senses are passionately keen. They want the things they like far more desperately than grown-ups; they detest the things they do not like far more violently. Yet we, cold and sagacious, or merely arbitrary, are always interfering with a child's desires.

"Only eat one piece." "No more now." "You may have it after dinner." "Eat what is on your plate." "Take this medicine at once!"—thus do the arbiters of fate dictate to this child.

They must wear what is given them; eat what is given them; take, generally, what is given them, or go without.

As for liberty, that basis of all high happiness, children have none. They may be docile or rebellious, but in either case they have ever upon them the pressure of another's will. The docile ones get the pleasure of commendation, and the rebellious ones, occasionally, the pleasure of partial and temporary independence; but then comes punishment, and, what is worse, disapproval.

Consider the atmosphere of constant criticism in which our children live. They are subject to the most intrusive personal examination and comment.

Misunderstanding does not promote happiness; yet childhood is a state of chronic misunderstanding. The child does not understand the things about him, the people, and their purposes. He is always questioning, and, all too often, being snubbed. As to understanding him—trying to get the child's point of view, to allow for his personal equation and good intentions—how rarely it is done!

Children grow up as best they may, under conditions of misunderstanding, criticism, questioning, interference, dictation, compulsion, and arbitrary punishment. Some of them are fairly happy; a few are truly and fully happy; but the majority of them long to "grow up" and enjoy life as their elders do!

# Chronological List of Sources

## 1909

"How Home Conditions React Upon the Family." *American Journal of Sociology*, Vol. 14, No. 5 (March): 592-605.
"The Man-Made Family." *The Forerunner*, Vol. 1, No. 2 (December): 19-23.

## 1910

"Prize Children." *The Forerunner*, Vol. 1, No. 7 (May): 10-11.
"The New Motherhood." *The Forerunner*, Vol. 1, No. 14 (December): 17-18.

## 1911

"Does a Man Support His Wife?" *The Forerunner*, Vol. 2, No. 9 (September): 240-246.
"Names—Especially Women's." *The Forerunner*, Vol. 2, No. 10 (October): 261-263.

## 1912

"Alimony." *The Forerunner*, Vol. 3, No. 3 (March): 82.
"Is There a Double Standard in Filial Duty?" *The Forerunner*, Vol. 3, No. 11 (November): 297-298.

## 1913

"My Ancestors." *The Forerunner*, Vol. 4, No. 3 (March): 73-75.
"Education for Motherhood." *The Forerunner*, Vol. 4, No. 10 (October): 259-262.
"Illegitimate Children." *The Forerunner*, Vol. 4, No. 11 (November): 295-297.

## 1914

"Wanted—Young Girl to Mind Baby and Do Light Housework." *The Forerunner*, Vol. 5, No. 4 (April): 88-89.

"These Proud Fathers." *The Forerunner*, Vol. 5, No. 5 (May): 129-130.
"Competing with Men." *The Forerunner*, Vol. 5, No. 7 (July): 193-194.

## 1915

"My Mother Right or Wrong." *The Forerunner*, Vol. 6, No. 2 (February): 45.
"Birth Control." *The Forerunner*, Vol. 6, No. 7 (July): 177-180.
"Without a Husband." *The Forerunner*, Vol. 6, No. 12 (December): 314.
"The Power of the Farm Wife." *The Forerunner*, Vol. 6, No. 12 (December): 315-319.

## 1916

"The Honor of Bearing His Name" (*The Forerunner*, Vol. 7, No. 2 (February): 46-47)
"Is Childhood Happy?" (*The Forerunner*, Vol. 7, No. 5 (May): 118)

# Index